Invest in Europe Now!

WHY EUROPE'S MARKETS WILL OUTPERFORM THE U.S. IN THE COMING YEARS

David R. Kotok
Vincenzo Sciarretta

WILEY

John Wiley & Sons, Inc.

Published by John Wiley & Sons, Inc., Hoboken, New Jersey.

Published simultaneously in Canada.

For general information on our other products and services or for technical support, please contact our Customer Care Department within the United States at (800) 762-2974, outside the United States at (317) 572-3993 or fax (317) 572-4002.

Wiley also publishes its books in a variety of electronic formats. Some content that appears in print may not be available in electronic books. For more information about Wiley products, visit our web site at www.wiley.com.

Library of Congress Cataloging-in-Publication Data:
Kotok, David.
    Invest in Europe now! : why Europe's markets will outperform the US in the coming years / David Kotok, Vincenzo Sciarretta.
        p. cm.
    Includes bibliographical references and index.
    ISBN 978-0-470-54701-4 (cloth)
    1. Investments–Europe. I. Sciarretta, Vincenzo. II. Title.
    HG5422.K68 2010
    330.94–dc22

                                                                    2009049438

Printed in the United States of America

10 9 8 7 6 5 4 3 2 1

To the memory of my mother, Sheva C. Kotok (1918–2008), mentor and teacher of English and math, whose reminder of "edit, edit, edit; proofread, proofread, proofread" will guide me all of my days.

David Kotok

To my wife, Babbila, and my first three children, Rocco, Alessandra, and Aurora. Yes, the obvious is sometimes the essence of life.

Vincenzo Sciarretta

Contents

Foreword

The argument is compelling. As the global economy emerges from the crisis, it is time to assess how structural changes affect investment decisions. The book zeroes in on two regions: the European Union (EU) and the United States. It takes a historical perspective on the evolution of the markets and methodically shows why, in the aftermath of the financial crisis, the equity investment pendulum is set to swing in favor of the EU. The analysis is couched in a discussion between two friends who have debated over a decade the regional advantages and drawbacks of the past 25 years—years dominated by deregulation, privatization, and globalization.

The first part of the book anchors the macroeconomic framework and lays out the argument regarding where to invest. In doing so, it discusses the success of the euro and makes a euro-bullish case relative to the dollar; it reviews the making of the EU single market, through both the institutional and policy lenses, and analyzes the ensuing convergence and integration of EU financial markets; and it briskly walks the reader through the labyrinth of taxation and evolution of stock markets.

Once the reader knows where to invest, the book guides him or her on how to invest. It examines investment tools, most notably low-cost exchange-traded-funds (ETFs) as an attractive option for investing in Europe. The reader is then equipped to conquer the more technically oriented second part of the book. This is a must-read for any investor interested in the EU. It offers detailed analyses of successful investment strategies as it examines valuations and discusses emerging Europe. To round off the discussion and allow the reader to assess all viewpoints, the third part of the book relates conversations the authors have had on this very subject with well-known market players.

For those who believed in the euro experiment all along, the premise of the book is sweet; for the die-hard euro skeptics, it is challenging; for yours truly, the book offers a wonderful intellectual smorgasbord—evocative of my native country, Norway—for picking and choosing. The reader need not agree with the book's broad conclusions, but may want to focus, along with policymakers, on the discussions related to the hard policy choices confronting the United States, or on the macro issues of currencies. Alternatively, the investor might want to dwell on investment strategies right away, or simply settle for the opinions voiced by the analysts whose views the authors solicited. In sum, the book offers an excellent investment discussion, tight in analysis, rich in details, and accessible to all.

—Kathleen Stephansen, Chief Economist and
Managing Director at Aladdin Capital Holdings, LLC

Preface

This book is written for investors. It seeks to provoke thought about asset allocation between the United States and Europe. It would have looked much different several years ago. Then, the United States was viewed as the most transparent, most dependable, best-regulated, most liquid, and most trusted capital market in the world.

That has changed. The United States gave the world Madoff, Stanford, Nadel, and others of their ilk. That scarred and damaged the image of the supervisory prowess of U.S. agencies like the Securities and Exchange Commission. The United States shattered world confidence when the ratings agencies downgraded trillions in so-called AAA securities. Washington caused dislocations and distrust when the U.S. government bailed out its federal agencies such as Fannie Mae and Freddie Mac. The errors of their ways have subsequently been revealed to cost the U.S. taxpayers billions. Securities of those agencies, such as their preferred stocks, collapsed in value, even though they had been held by banks and institutions as the highest-quality instruments, according to governing regulations.

Perhaps the greatest devastation occurred as the world watched as Lehman Brothers failed, even though it was a primary dealer with the Federal Reserve. The last primary dealer to fail was Drexel Burnham, many years ago. Readers must not casually dismiss the absolute damage to the global image of the Federal Reserve when it effectively failed to police the risk-taking behavior of one of its primary dealers. The designation of primary-dealer status is rare in the United States and requires extensive effort on the part of the dealer to become qualified.

Lehman Brothers' demise was an unexpected and unmitigated disaster. Its fallout must not be underestimated. The world's stock markets lost 25 percent of their collective value during the five weeks following the failure of Lehman. Bond market spreads widened to unprecedented levels, and many market sectors completely seized and froze up; others operated with huge, dysfunctional pricing levels.

Ethical lapses during this crisis period were and are a great embarrassment to the United States. The Federal Reserve Bank of New York had Lehman's CEO on its board of directors during the period following the Bear Stearns affair and as the Fed was altering its rules to provide Lehman and the other primary dealers with special new lending facilities. Subsequent revelations showed the present U.S. Treasury Secretary was a tax scofflaw while he was the sitting president of the New York Fed during the financial crisis. The New York Fed board chairman traded stock in Goldman Sachs while his Federal Reserve regional bank was involved in the financial bailout with that company and other firms who were indebted to it. The lack of ethical behavior at the New York Fed under then-president Timothy Geithner is appalling in the eyes of these authors.

This book will set forth the debate on a number of issues that lead to the conclusion that Europe is ascending to a preferred allocation choice over the United States. We will talk about the policy applications that have changed how the European Union and Eurozone have developed and how comparisons can be made against U.S. developments in the same historical period. We'll examine the nature of the Federal Reserve and the European Central Bank and their respective monetary-policy frameworks. We will compare fiscal policies and taxation. We will talk about the relationship between the dollar and the euro. And we will discuss the stocks and stock markets that may look appealing to a U.S. investor interested in Europe.

The genesis of this book came about a decade ago. Vincenzo Sciarretta and David Kotok were riding across Italy from Rome to a small town named Montorio al Vomano, in the province of Teramo in the Abruzzo region of southern Italy. Sciarretta was interviewing Kotok about the period after the tech-stock bubble burst. Readers will see the value of Sciarretta's interviews in the "guru" chapters of this book. Sciarretta's fiancée, Babbila, drove. Mutual friend and University of Pennsylvania professor Peter Steiner listened as Sciarretta argued that European stocks and European markets had a positive outlook, in spite of the fact that the character and structure of the European Union were uncertain.

On the other hand, Kotok argued that the Eurozone was untried and, although he was hopeful about it, there was still time to shift asset weights from the United States to Europe. Kotok believed that the likelihood of an increasingly center-left form of government would impose higher costs and taxes on businesses in the newly developed and expanding European Economic Community. Kotok also believed that the price/earnings multiple on European stocks should be lower than that in the United States, because the United States had more of a free-market climate and was more entrepreneurial and risk-taking. Kotok argued that the United States would grow faster than Europe. Kotok's case suggested that U.S. stock markets deserved a higher premium than European stocks of companies in the same or similar businesses. This premium was measured in the traditional way, by price/earnings, price/sales, and price/book ratios.

After this journey, Kotok and Sciarretta remained close friends over the years. They visited each other regularly. Kotok watched as Sciarretta married Babbila, and their family grew. When Kotok and Sciarretta were able, they jointly attended Global Interdependence Center functions in Europe, which provided them the opportunity to remain personally in touch. Kotok is the program chair of the Global Interdependence Center, a Philadelphia-based monetary and trade think tank. The Europe versus United States debate between Kotok and Sciarretta continued throughout the decade.

Sciarretta never wavered. He took a longer-term view and still believes that European stocks remain cheap. His journalistic experience, writing about stock markets and businesses for many years, and his deep, local exposure to European markets give him comfort in his position.

It is Kotok who has changed his view of the world in light of the financial crisis and the policy actions that evolved in the Bush administration, with particular emphasis on the final two Bush years. Kotok's metamorphosis was completed with the lurching leftward of the Obama administration after it took office.

After a decade of debate between friends, for the first time, Kotok now agrees with Sciarretta and thinks that Europe has more potential in the future than the United States. That's not because the European normal growth rate will accelerate to some new, higher level than it has experienced in the last decade. Rather, it is the policies of the United States, which are reducing the United States' outlook for growth and bringing it down to a new and slower growth level, in an era in which the United States, too, will function as a social-democratic form of government.

Kotok believes that the United States is developing a broad "industrial policy" and has already done that in sufficient depth to impact about half of the U.S. economy. Readers who are not familiar with the term industrial policy should recognize it from the political debates that have occurred over the course of a century in the United States and elsewhere in the world. Essentially, an industrial policy means some form of governmental direction and intervention into a mixed economy. Industrial policies are applied in lieu of, or in order to alter, traditional free-trading or free-market policies.

The United States recently has grown in the use of industrial policies. Americans have seen them for years in agriculture. In the United States, the agriculture industrial policy brought Americans things like the huge federal subsidies for ethanol or the tariffs and protectionism for sugar. In recent times, and more so since the financial crisis has evolved, the industrial-policy sectors targeted by the federal government have included housing and mortgage finance, banking, capital markets, health care, and automobiles and their related suppliers, just to name a few.

In other words, directives and influences from Washington now govern over half the U.S. economy in an interventionist way. This makes the United States more like the other countries in the world that engage in industrial policies. Government has removed, or is removing, the free-market-oriented structures of the past.

Kotok's view is that this eliminates the arguments for any risk premium attached to U.S. stocks. Essentially, we are growing more like Europe and will be practicing a form of mixed economy, and, Kotok asserts, so far we are doing this poorly.

Over time, the European Union (EU) has developed a fairly comprehensive although sometimes cumbersome structural framework by which the EU advances its economies and applies its industrial policies. (We are thinking specifically of the Treaty of Lisbon, signed in December 2007.) Europeans know how to be social democrats.

In the United States, this process is much newer and more fragmented. Americans are rank beginners when it comes to being social democrats, and they are going to learn the hard way. That means any premium attributable to U.S. stocks needs to be reexamined. If Americans are going to be more like the EU, if our policies are going to be similar to the Europeans', if our social benefits are going to be ratcheted up to levels that rival theirs, and if the costs are going to be borne by the U.S. economy, as European costs are borne by their economies, then Americans must view the valuations of U.S. securities on an equal footing with Europe.

Under those assumptions, Sciarretta's argument that European stocks are cheap relative to U.S. stocks becomes valid. Kotok draws the same conclusion, albeit for a different reason than Sciarretta.

Sciarretta is very confident in his favorable view of Europe. He's a European. He lives within the EU. He uses the euro. He has examined these issues for many, many years and is comfortable with his position. Sciarretta will make his case for stocks in Europe in several chapters of this book. He will outline his valuation metrics and offer readers some backtesting of them. Readers may then judge the value of these metrics for themselves.

Kotok is less comfortable and less secure with his views. He doesn't know how to be a social democrat but is trying to learn. He developed his professional experience examining freer and more open markets and has only recently come to the conclusions articulated in this book.

Kotok isn't sure whether the political pendulum in the United States could reverse and swing back and away from an industrial policy that is very interventionist and very directed by the federal government. If, in fact, the post-Obama pendulum swings away from its present left-of-center position, then, Kotok argues, U.S. markets could again become a better bargain than European markets. That caution admitted, it is Kotok's view that reversal away from industrial policies is not likely to happen soon in the United States. Hence, at the moment, Kotok's view is not sanguine about the business and investment outlook for the United States relative to that for Europe. Readers will find this view articulated in the various chapters of this book.

Acknowledgments

The authors wish to acknowledge the great deal of help received from various parties over the course of the development of this book. They have decided to prepare separate acknowledgments.

Kotok wishes specifically to thank colleagues within his firm who assisted him: Michael Comes, Peter Demirali, Daisy Lopez, Michael McNiven, John Mousseau, Sam Santiago, Phyllis Streit, Julie Takeda, Nelly Vidro, and Alexandra Warzecha.

Kotok wishes especially to mention Kathleen Stephansen, a skilled and thoughtful economist, who has assisted in research and acted as a reader, and who agreed to write the foreword for the book. Kathleen's input has been enormously helpful in the entire macro section of the book and especially in the chapter on convergence and integration. She recently became the chief economist and a managing director at Aladdin Capital.

Kotok also wishes to thank Matthew Hougan, who is the director of ETF analysis for IndexUniverse.com. Matt is also a consultant to Cumberland Advisors for specific research assistance on ETFs. He was the primary research source for the chapter on exchange-traded funds. Matt is a recognized world expert on this subject, and his help with that chapter is greatly appreciated by the authors.

Kotok also needs to acknowledge his attorney, Jeffrey Kramer, for legal assistance in matters involving the authors and the publisher. These issues included the fact that Kotok is a U.S. citizen and Sciarretta is a citizen of Italy.

Kotok also wishes to acknowledge the assistance of Robert Ophele, Director General Operations of the Banque de France, who helped as a reader of the chapter on the euro versus the dollar. However, the opinions in this book are those of the authors and not the Banque de France. Robert Ophele was particularly helpful in checking and noting factual errors in drafts and directing Kotok to sources for data.

Finally, Kotok must thank his co-author, Vincenzo Sciarretta, who pushed him for years to partner with him in the writing of this book, and who finally succeeded.

Sciarretta wishes to thank David Kotok for accepting the idea of this book. He probably underestimated what a lot of work a book is; otherwise, he would have certainly dismissed the invitation. But, to my great surprise, he threw himself into the project. All of a sudden, he organized a team around it and started working on it with the vigor and energy of a man who had something to prove. Having to run his own trading firm—Cumberland Advisors—in addition to being a regular contributor for CNBC and serving as a program chairman of the Global Interdependence Center, I found him sending e-mails in the heart of the night, or losing his temper because he was swamped with the "damned book." It is in his work ethic that David is a role model to me.

I also thank Alex Warzecha, who coordinated our work and had to handle my accumulated delays.

As an Italian, writing a book in English was a big, big challenge. Charley Sweet, our copyeditor, helped keep my writing under control.

Thanks to FactSet's team in Milan, which provided some of the data. They not only have a magnificent database, but Christian De Angelis was always there to pick up my calls when I needed additional explanations. And if he was on holiday, there was Roberta Barone to answer my questions.

Massimiliano Malandra ran his computer ragged, backtesting traditional investment strategies on Eurozone historical data. His abilities were essential in that chapter.

My only regret about the book is that I could not include an interview with any of the professionals who comprise Morgan Stanley's European Equity Team. I tried, but I failed. Yet, the group enabled me to republish some of their in-depth tables and charts. I am grateful, because they produce excellent research. However, I should make clear that, although Morgan Stanley's European Equity Team and Ufficio Studi Mediobanca allowed to reproduce some of their material, this does not mean they are responsible for any of the ideas or conclusions presented in this book.

I cannot finish without one big set of additional thanks to the "gurus," whose interviews constitute the last block of chapters. They were generous with their time, and they provided invaluable and thought-provoking points of view. Their caliber is outstanding. Thanks to Marc Faber, Mark Mobius, William Clark, Felix Zulauf, Ken Fisher, Ed Yardeni, Bob McKee, Emanuele Ravano, Catherine Mann, and François-Xavier Chevallier.

Both authors want to acknowledge the help of the folks at John Wiley & Sons, Inc.: David Pugh, Laura Walsh, and Kelly O'Connor. Without good publishers insisting on clarity and giving advice, books would not come to pass in readable form.

Disclaimer

The materials contained herein represent the opinions of the authors, contributors, and editors and should not be construed as a recommendation to buy or sell securities. Nothing contained in this book is to be considered as the rendering of any form of investment advice. Readers are responsible for obtaining such advice from their own investment advisors.

All information published herein is gathered from sources that are thought to be reliable; the authors, contributors, and editors are not responsible for errors.

Introduction

Reaching an investment decision and following through with the deployment of monies is an age-old process. As long as we've had money and accumulated wealth, men and women have struggled with the decision of how to invest it. There are many techniques used to evaluate investments in general, and particularly with stocks and stock markets. All of them are subject to debate, discussion, analysis, and examination.

Stocks represent ownership shares in companies that do business in countries and regions. Companies also have a favored or home-based currency, reflecting their national identity. Furthermore, companies employ people. People have their cultural differences, natural language preferences established at their birth, and various forms of business structure. When an investor chooses a currency, a region, a country, and a company, he or she is also choosing the people who work, manage, develop, and direct the policies of the company.

This book is focused on these choices investors make. In targeting the United States, Europe and, particularly, the Eurozone within Europe, it attempts to point out the differences between the Eurozone and the United States as they have developed in recent times. While we may observe some longer-term strategic ways to evaluate stocks, the authors are focused on differences that we believe have been and are occurring between these two large economic regions.

Invest in Europe Now! is told from two unique perspectives, that of David Kotok, an American who is the cofounder and Chief Investment Officer of Cumberland Advisors, and Vincenzo Sciarretta, a journalist from Italy who has written for the main financial weekly magazines in the country. In using the perspective of an author in

1

Europe and the United States, we seek to outline the best ways to take advantage of the rapidly shifting global environment.

Thus, this book is divided into three parts. In the first part, co-author Kotok focuses on the macro differences between the Eurozone and the United States. One of the major arguments of this book is that the currency under the supervision of the European Central Bank and now deployed in most of Europe is rooted in principles and policies that will make it a more deeply reliable currency than the currency of the United States. This is a conjectural argument to make, because no one knows for sure how the future will play out. The chapter "Euro versus Dollar" argues the case in favor of the euro and against the dollar.

The first part of the book also talks about the benefits that have been attained in Europe since the Eurozone was created and the European Union established. It discusses successes that occurred as barriers have fallen and financial efficiencies have occurred. Those benefits continue to accrue as the process of integration and convergence develops in the European Union and, specifically, in the countries that are now newly admitted into the Eurozone. The evolution of European stock exchanges demonstrates this process.

We both expect these trends to persist, because more and more countries and more and more people will accept the euro as their basic currency. They will accept the business structure of the European Union as the way in which they operate their economic lives. This is to be contrasted with changes in the United States that have occurred under the Bush and Obama administrations. The United States seems to have lost many of the characteristics of its original free-market entrepreneurial system and moved toward more of a social-democratic system. A chapter on taxation helps clarify these differences.

For American investors there is also a separate chapter on exchange-traded funds (ETFs) and how they might be helpful in investing in Europe. (As a side note, we are grateful to Matt Hougan for lending his expertise in the formulation of this chapter.) The chapter also talks about the principles surrounding ETFs, which can be applied anywhere in the world. The specifics of ETFs that can get American investors involved in the Eurozone are also described.

In the second part of the book, Sciarretta takes the lead, discussing successful strategies, valuations, and methodologies to deploy funds in the Eurozone. Sciarretta brings useful tools and the statistical results of back testing to argue ways in which funds might be deployed in Europe. (In addition to individual indicators, combinations of them were also backtested.) He emphasizes an individual stock-picking style, which differentiates him from Kotok, whose firm's stock style focuses on the use of ETFs. (As a side note, Kotok's company, Cumberland Advisors, does not employ single stocks in its investment-management strategy.)

Sciarretta has used time-tested methods that have a long history in the United States. With the assistance of Massimiliano Malandra, he was able to run statistical samples on a range of indicators of the relative performance of stocks. Details of those tests and the multi-year periods covered are found in the chapters of the second part of this book. These strategies will be helpful to investors who seek to pick individual stocks in Europe rather than indexes or baskets using ETFs.

The last part of the book is made up of the "Guru" chapters. In this part, the journalist Sciarretta interviews several substantial, reputable, prominent investors and professionals and seeks their views on the best investment opportunities in Europe and abroad.

Although these gurus don't all necessarily agree with us or one another, they all believe that Europe is very well positioned to capitalize on the opening up of China and the boom in emerging markets. After all, a stock's price at any given moment reflects the attitude, approach, and valuation of all the investors who are paying attention to the news and events surrounding that particular stock at that particular instant. Those are diverse views. Different people see the world in different ways. However, the price of the stock is the clearing price. It reflects known sentiment and emotion, psychology as well as factual and numerical data. It all comes together in a price, and that is a dynamic entity that is changing every single second. The "guru" chapters were designed to reflect that perception, because the authors have asked the interviewees to think in a strategic way as they share their views of stock markets, companies, and regions.

Of course, investing is never that simple. There are always risks, which we also discuss with the "gurus." An example: The benign cycle between Eastern Europe and core Europe may turn into a vicious circle for a while. Yet bargains do exist, as you'll read in the conversation with Mark Mobius. Banks are a question mark. A very large sector in Europe—much larger than in the United States—they may not excel in the aftermath of the 2008 crisis.

What about real opportunities? As we write, the European Union's population is passing the 500 million mark. It's such a large block of advanced economies, yet it's an undiscovered gem for most investors. You do not read many cover stories on European stocks. You do not find a lot of Europe-focused books on Amazon. Few are paying attention to Eurozone stocks. But the opportunities are there, and the "gurus" helped us to single them out. Read and discover them for yourself.

This book may or may not offer investors a magic formula to a profitable future. None of us are smart enough to know the future. But, what we can offer is an assembled collection of indicators to follow, instruments to use, traps to avoid, and viewpoints to listen to that will help investors formulate alternative investment options in this ever-changing, global world.

PART

I

MACRO ISSUES

CHAPTER 1

Euro Versus Dollar

Many shall be restored that now are fallen, and many shall fall that now are in honor.

—Horace

Launching a new currency for a large economic area is an extraordinary event in the history of monetary economics. The euro area certainly qualifies as large in economic size, as measured by GDP, in population size (hundreds of millions of people), and in political configuration, as it encompasses many nation-states with diverse languages and cultures. History will show the introduction of the euro as a grand and unique experiment in monetary economics.

Euro skeptics existed before the actual launch of the currency. The doubters cited a multitude of reasons why this grand experiment would fail. So far, however, the result has been success, and the world is witnessing the emergence of a strong, reliable, and viable reserve currency. This chapter offers some observations about that evolution and opinions about its continued favorable prospects.

Creation of the Euro and Transfer of Currencies

Getting to a single currency in Europe was a century-long task that first required several catastrophes.[1] One could argue that it started with the collapse of Czarist Russia, coincident with World War I. This led to the division of Eastern and Western Europe. The Weimar Republic's hyperinflation and subsequent demise led to the rise of Nazism. From the final chapters of World War II came the subsequent global dominance by the United States. The largesse of the United States, with the Marshall Plan and the rebuilding of Europe, was followed by four decades of internal European dialogue. 1992 was a special year. The Treaty of Maastricht, signed on February 7, 1992, was coincident with the peaceful emergence of an independent central Europe and the demise of communist USSR domination.

European countries decided to formally set aside war and to coalesce toward a single economic unit. In 1991, they seriously started the contractual attempt to achieve a single currency. After a thousand years of enmity, France and Germany engaged in true *rapprochement*. The 1992 Maastricht Treaty set the Eurozone admission criteria regarding national budget deficits and actual rates of inflation.[2]

The goal of this new "hard" currency was to be dependable and reliable. The condition that the currency could not be manipulated by a single national government led the target list of accomplishments. Devaluation as a single-country option was eliminated. The new euro was to be "inflation-proof."

The Maastricht Treaty required ratification by its members. That process took place in the decade of the 1990s. The final formulas and currency exchange rates among the original eleven members of the Eurozone were not completed until the end of that decade, in 1998. Of the original fifteen countries that determined to form a European economic community, to be named the European Union (EU), only the UK, Denmark, and Sweden decided not to join the currency union.

On January 1, 1999, the virtual euro began to trade in eleven countries. It was an immediate success. As agreed, three years later, on January 1, 2002, the paper euro replaced the national currencies of the then twelve countries. The European Central Bank (ECB) was born. It was charged with the responsibility of maintaining price stability, which it defined as an annual inflation rate of under but close to 2 percent in the medium term. It is an independent, separate body, above the political power of any single national government. It has its own governing council. The terms of its construction

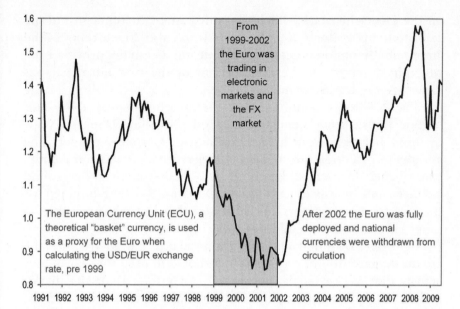

From
1999-2002
the Euro was
trading in
electronic
markets and
the FX
market

The European Currency Unit (ECU), a
theoretical "basket" currency, is used
as a proxy for the Euro when
calculating the USD/EUR exchange
rate, pre 1999

After 2002 the Euro was fully
deployed and national
currencies were withdrawn from
circulation

Figure 1.1 Euro Declines Rapidly Against the Dollar, then Rebounds Strongly
Source: Bloomberg and Cumberland Advisors.

are defined in a treaty to which Eurozone countries subscribed. Only unanimous consent can change those terms.

The early stages of the euro (see Figure 1.1) showed a rapid decline in value against the dollar. From its January 1, 1999, opening price of $1.17 to its low of $0.84, the euro seemed to be a candidate for freefall. Euro skeptics had many reasons for claiming the euro would not succeed and that the experiment in monetary union would fail. They were wrong.

Euro skeptics argued that economic, political, and capital market forces were behind the euro's weakness.[3] Their attention was misdirected, and they may have missed the significance of the conversion of cash balances, which were prevalent throughout Europe and in other parts of the world.

Early studies, including a 2001 study by two economists from the University of Munich and published by the National Bureau of Economic Research (NBER), showed large hoards of cash that had been used in the underground economy in Western Europe, Eastern Europe, and other parts of the world.[4] The NBER study focused only on the Deutsche mark, which was a dominant currency in Europe prior to the introduction of the euro. It was also the currency of the largest single national economy in Europe. Germany provided the lynchpin currency in the composition of the new euro that was replacing the Deutsche mark.

The NBER study argued that the excess balances above and beyond transactional demand exceeded 100 billion D-marks. Many of those balances were located outside of Germany proper. The authors of this book investigated currency balances in several countries during this period. It was clear to us that large underground balances and hoards of cash in lire, D-marks, etc. were targeted for transfer to the new euro. We surmised that the same was true in other countries that we did not visit.

In order to understand this transfer, one has to visualize the circumstances. An underground hoard of cash used for gray-money activity that was originally positioned in German Deutsche marks, Italian lira, Spanish pesetas, or French francs had to be transferred out of those currencies, because they would become the euro. It needed to be done surreptitiously and over a period of time.[5]

The target currencies that were deep enough to absorb such a large transfer were quite limited. They were the Japanese yen, the U.S. dollar, the British pound, and the Swiss franc. Transfers had to be done in relatively small sums and on a continuing basis. Remember, lots of cash was being moved, and it was being done from an illegal or underground gray-money business perspective. Therefore, it had to be done in repeated transactions of smaller amounts. Also remember that each transfer constituted a sale of the new euro and the purchase of U.S. dollars, Swiss francs, or something else.

Among the target currencies, the most difficult one for Europeans was the Swiss franc. This was due to the fact that cash transactions were being followed closely within Europe. There was also national governmental scrutiny, both by the eleven countries that made up the new Eurozone and by the Swiss banking authorities.

The Japanese yen at the time was a suspect currency because of the weakness in the Japanese economic system, which had persisted for years and showed no signs of recovery. That left the British pound, which received some inflows, and last but most important, the U.S. dollar.

The U.S. dollar was a deeply liquid and large enough world market. It had sufficient transactional capability and probably became the focal point of transfer during the pre-2002 informal period when gray-money balances were transferring out of the original eleven (twelve, with Greece joining in 2001) national currencies. When the virtual euro was launched, there were only three years left for those transfers.

The pace accelerated through 2001 until January 2002 when, with the successful launch of the paper euro, the national currencies of twelve countries were withdrawn and replaced. At the same time, the process of withdrawing gray-money hoards from dollars, pounds, etc. and replacing them with the euro commenced vigorously.

It took only a few months to reverse the trend of dollar strength and euro weakness. The euro skeptics, who had argued against the euro in economic terms, were discredited.

Following the 2002 launch of the full euro, including paper currency and coins, the large cash balances and hoards were rebuilt in euros. This caused the selling of dollars and buying of euros. After the start in 2002 the process accelerated. The more the euro persisted and was accepted, the stronger it got. We can see that the extreme weakness against the U.S. dollar coincided with the launching of the paper euro (Figure 1.2).

By 2003, the euro was a full-fledged currency, standing on its own. The European Central Bank's policies and the implementation of same were going to determine its value, just as the ongoing

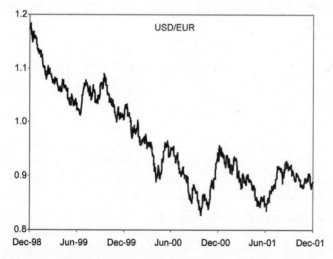

Figure 1.2 Euro Weak During Virtual Period January 1999 to January 2002

Source: Bloomberg and Cumberland Advisors.

policies and implementation of the Federal Reserve would determine the value of the U.S. dollar.

Starting in 2003, the world was about to witness a strategic monetary race between the euro and the dollar, between the ECB and the Federal Reserve. Never before had such a large enterprise as a supranational currency in a major economic body been launched. Eleven national governments agreed to give up their sovereignty over their currencies and cede it to a central bank. National decision making was limited. The euro was and is a grand experiment in the history of monetary economics.[6]

Success of the Euro, 10 Years Later

We can fast-forward to the present and see that the euro is a resounding success. After ten years, the eleven countries have now expanded to sixteen (Figure 1.3). Additional EU countries are in the Exchange Rate Mechanism (ERM) as they prepare to adopt the euro.

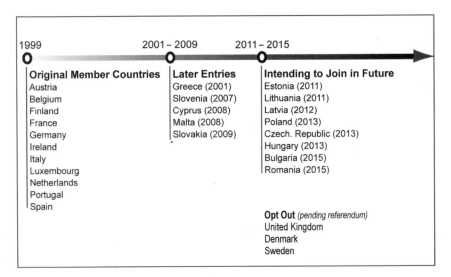

Figure 1.3   Expansion of the Eurozone
Source: "The Euro Area," European Central Bank, www.ecb.int/euro/intro/html/map.en.html; "Where Eastern Europeans Stand on Euro Adoption," Thomson Financial, www.forbes.com/feeds/afx/2009/01/22/afx5951139.html; January 2009 Reuters poll of analysts on euro adoption dates.

Latest estimates indicate the euro constitutes approximately 25 percent of the world's reserves.[7] That's not too bad for an upstart currency only 10 years old. The U.S. dollar share of the world's reserves is down to about 65 percent.[8] The other 10 percent consists of currencies from the rest of the world.

On the subject of financial markets, one has to look at both the components of the stock market, which this book does in detail, and at the world's bond markets when considering how the array of currencies now interact in the world. One can see that indebtedness issued in the euro is roughly equal in size to indebtedness issued in the U.S. dollar. These two have become the dominant debt currencies of the globe. The British pound and the Japanese yen have secondary roles, and other OECD countries have much smaller shares. Of the approximately 85 trillion U.S. dollar equivalent of global indebtedness, about $24 trillion is issued in euros and $33 trillion in U.S. dollars. Taking only international bonds, about $10.5 trillion is issued in euros and $8.5 trillion in U.S. dollars (Figure 1.4).[9]

During its first decade the euro has continued to strengthen against the dollar as both a virtual and paper currency. Outstanding

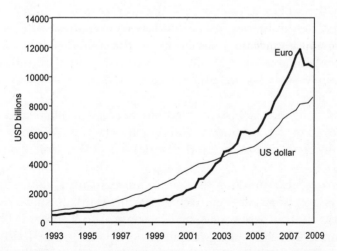

Figure 1.4 International Debt Issued in Euros and U.S. Dollars Is Roughly Equal

Note: Amounts outstanding of international bonds and notes by type, sector, and currency in billions of U.S. dollars.

Source: Bank for International Settlements *BIS Quarterly Review*, June 2009.

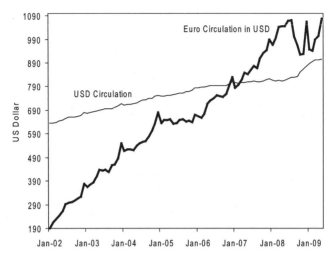

Figure 1.5   Global Cash Outstanding in Euros Is Greater than in U.S. Dollars

Source: Federal Reserve Bank of St. Louis, European Central Bank, and Cumberland Advisors.

cash in the world denominated in euros is now a larger amount than that denominated in U.S. dollars (see Figure 1.5). Such cash is utilized in legitimate transactions in the global economic arena, as one would expect. Cash is also used in underground activity. Gray-money balances are now denominated more in euros than in U.S. dollars.

The euro has achieved credibility, respectability, and power in circulation far beyond anyone's expectations. When it comes to currencies of choice around the globe, the U.S. dollar is morphing into second place behind the euro. When it comes to trade, the euro is also holding its own: The euro area share of trade (imports + exports) has gained relative to the U.S. share. In 2000 it stood at 14.9 percent versus the U.S. share at 15.9 percent. Through mid-year 2009, the euro area share of global trade held steady at 14.8 percent, while that of the U.S. share fell to 11.7 percent.[10] When it comes to outstanding bond indebtedness, it is fair to say that the U.S. dollar and the euro are in a tie. As this book argues in other chapters, stock market trends are likely to follow this pattern.

Central Banks: The ECB Versus the Fed

Let's address the construction of the central banks. Eurozone monetary policy is directed by the governing council of the European Central Bank. Inflation is the primary enemy of the ECB. The currency's buying power is mandated to be kept as stable as possible. Inflation is targeted (below but close to 2 percent) and monetary policies are directed first and foremost at the maintenance of a strong and reliable currency. The ECB's monetary-policy strategy includes a quantitative definition of price stability and a two-pillar approach to the analysis of the risks to price stability (an economic and monetary analysis).[11] Europeans have a long history. Clearly, they do not trust the political construction of their governments. Over the course of a thousand years they have watched the value of currency erode through inflation. They have watched governments confiscate wealth. They are suspicious of government, and they have good reasons.

The formulation of the European Central Bank was directed at providing Europeans a safe and reliable currency in which they could transact their monetary affairs. The purpose was to define the characteristics of a medium of exchange in which they could hold their currency and not worry about rapid inflation, which would erode its value.[12] Monetary policy was aimed at meeting the classic economic definition of money, that it be a way to "store value." The euro was quickly accepted after 2002, thereby meeting the third requirement of a currency, which is to be a unit of account. These are the three things necessary for a currency to succeed:

1. Be a medium of exchange
2. Store value
3. Be a unit of account

The euro now meets all three tests.

The political construction of the European Central Bank is resolved, accepted, and clearly determined in a way in which that central bank's independence is maintained. The ECB has become increasingly credible during the decade of its activities.

When we look to the dollar, we find a different construction underway. For years the dollar was paramount in the world. It was the preeminent currency and was viewed as qualified by all three standards. After the suspension of the Bretton Woods fixed-currency regime and the closure of the gold window under President Nixon, the U.S. dollar started to lose its luster.

As this is written, there are serious questions about the persistent and continuing value of the U.S. dollar vis-à-vis most other currencies in the world. Over time, the dollar has developed a reputation for bouts of weakness. Very few forecasts of a long-term nature view the dollar as the dominant, preeminent global currency for the next several decades. Many more forecasts focus on the euro and the construction of the ECB, which is keeping that currency strong.

In the United States, the Federal Reserve in the last few years has developed a reputation of being held hostage to U.S. politics, with regard to the makeup of its Board of Governors, its loss of policy independence, and problems with policy strategy. This has accelerated and intensified the suspicion about weakness in the U.S. dollar.

With regard to the current Board of Governors, at the time this book is written, the confirmation of two governors has been held up by the U.S. Senate Committee on Banking, led by Chairman Christopher Dodd (D-Connecticut), throughout the financial crisis of the last several years.[13] This has meant the Fed had to operate under a unanimity rule when it needed to deploy emergency decision making during the financial crisis.

Very few observers understand the difference between a unanimity rule and a supermajority rule. During the creation of the Federal Reserve rules as a response to the Great Depression in the 1930s, it was determined that the Board of Governors would make normal decisions with four of seven affirmative votes, but to invoke "emergent and exigent powers" would require five of seven votes. Never was it contemplated that there would only be five governors seated. When you have a supermajority rule, you allow room for dissent, debate, discussion, a record, and a narrative that can be examined and studied with respect to policy-making decisions.

Under a unanimity rule any governor has a veto. In fact, the records of the financial crisis indicate that the only emergency actions we know about coming from the Fed Board of Governors are those with five affirmative votes. We have no way of knowing about votes with four in favor and one dissenter. They were not recorded; no formal record exists. We have no way to know whether Chairman Bernanke, under pressure during those critical decision-making periods, was unable to obtain five votes. During crisis periods, failure to have agreement at the Fed may have exacerbated the disasters, including the Fed's primary-dealer difficulties involving Bear Stearns, Lehman Brothers, Merrill Lynch, and Countrywide.

With regard to the erosion of policy independence at the Fed, we look at the redefinition of the Federal Reserve's role under the Obama administration proposals. Under certain circumstances, the Treasury Secretary of the United States will have the power to veto a Federal Reserve action. If there is an action, the Fed will not be able to implement it until it receives written permission from the Secretary of the Treasury.

The Secretary of the Treasury in the United States is a cabinet official appointed by the President, reporting to the President, and meeting with the President on a weekly basis. Clearly, the U.S. central bank's independence is being undermined. Political forces in the United States continue to threaten other aspects of the Fed's activities and independence. And in the early months of the Obama administration, the Federal Reserve Board of Governors has continued to operate with two vacancies.

The authors of this book believe the long-term trend does not favor central-bank independence in the United States. Instead, it favors federal government intervention in monetary affairs. History is replete with examples of central-bank policy failure when the national government directs that policy.

This outcome doesn't always have to be extreme, as in the cases of the Weimar Republic or Zimbabwe. It can be a relative weakness. One currency can be more preferred than another currency. Part of that preference can be due to the political influences and directives that the national government imposes on its central bank. Sadly for the United States, the outlook for the Federal Reserve as an independent central bank of the United States is not sanguine. In sum, U.S. politics are set to permanently weaken the U.S. dollar.

Turning to the Fed's policy strategy, we believe that the central bank's two mandates are also a negative for the dollar. The Fed is supposed to control and restrain the rate of inflation. The Fed is also to maintain full employment and achieve maximum economic growth. These standards are conflicting, even though members of the Federal Reserve sometimes argue that they are consistent. They argue that inflation itself destroys growth and, therefore, by fighting inflation they will attempt to achieve the best level of economic growth. Recall, it was former Fed Chairman

Greenspan who introduced "risk management" as a policy strategy aimed at resolving the inconsistency of the two mandates.[14]

However you want to phrase the debate, the Federal Reserve faces a dual mandate. It has to fight inflation, and it has to stimulate growth. The process by which it determines priorities is a function of the U.S. political system. Contrast this with the European Central Bank and the euro, where the ECB's primary purpose is to keep inflation low and keep the currency dependable and reliable. Furthermore, the ECB does so with a stated mathematical target, so that all can measure its success. The Fed has no formal target, therefore no policy anchor.

Studies by central banks, including the Federal Reserve, indicate that inflation-targeting regimes are able to reduce the inflation risk premium in their financial markets when they are successful.[15] The reason is simple. Market players are able to access what the inflation target is, understand how it is measured, and, subsequently, determine whether the central bank is doing a good or bad job in achieving the results. Where there is no inflation target, there is a band of uncertainty that creeps into the pricing of financial assets. We call this the inflation risk premium. In the case of the United States, one can guess at the degree of inflation risk premium by measuring the spread between inflation-indexed Treasury securities (TIPS) and conventional Treasury securities in order to determine a market-based forecast of inflation and, hence, an inflation risk premium. Survey data is another way of estimating the inflation risk premium.

What does all this mean for stock market investors when they have to choose between two currencies? The same question can be asked in virtually any asset class. The answer is always the same.

If an investor is seeking to conserve the value of his or her investments, obtain growth, and endure minimal distortions in the accounting methodology used to report earnings and balance sheets of the various companies in which he or she invests, that investor seeks the more reliable currency. Inflation and a weaker currency have the tendency to distort the real economic value of a corporate entity. A company that is making money because of the change in the currency in which it reports its activities is not demonstrating unit growth, productivity, or reliable and dependable earnings that are understandable. That company's results are distorted through financial accounting; it is reporting profits because of changes in price levels due to inflation. Therefore, corporate inventory results are misstated. Debt payments or other accounting reports from the company have to reveal the impact of price changes. Companies manage their finances in currencies based upon whether the currencies that they choose can store value and are reliable. Otherwise, they have to engage in costly hedging operations because of changes in currency exchange ratios.[16]

Global Capital Reallocation Toward the Euro

Over a long period of time, currencies that hold their value become a more attractive investment domicile than weaker and more distrusted currencies. In the case of the euro, developments in its markets have led to more reliability of the euro and focused a global reallocation to it.

A good example of this can be seen in the aftermath of the global financial crisis. Here we have an opportunity to examine the banking sector and stock-market capitalization by currency and valuation that banks experienced in stock markets around the world.

In 1999, at the time the euro was launched, 24 U.S. banks were listed among the top 50 banks when ranked by total market capitalization.[17] Eleven continental European banks were on the list. So were seven British banks. The rest of the banks that made the top-50 list in market cap included six from Japan, one from Australia, and one from Hong Kong.

Compare those statistics with the spring of 2009. Of the top 50 banks in market cap, only 11 U.S. banks made the list.[18] This is a pronounced and dramatic decline from the period in which the euro was launched, ten years earlier. There were still eleven continental European banks in the top-50 list. Only three British banks made the cut.

Of the remaining, Japan could list four banks. There were many new faces, including six Chinese, five Canadian, four Australian, three Brazilian, one Russian, one Indian, and one bank from Hong Kong. The three largest banks in the world as measured by market cap were Chinese. Their combined market cap exceeded the total market value of the five largest U.S. banks.

The depth of the impact of the financial crisis in the United States was certainly a major force causing U.S. banking decline. Less recognized is the strength of the euro. It is probably largely responsible for the shift.

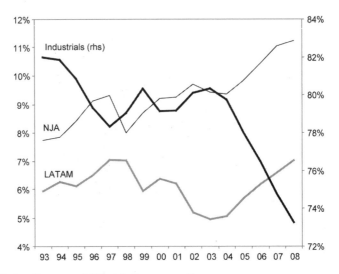

Figure 1.6   Shares of World Consumption
Source: IMF and OECD.

Economist David Hale has noted how the recent financial crisis has produced major changes in the global balance of financial power,[19] such as in the changes in bank market cap and the changing composition of global consumption (see Figure 1.6, which depicts the share of consumption by industrial countries relative to global consumption as ebbing, while that of emerging markets is rising, a trend that will likely intensify in years ahead).

The shift in the balance of financial power can be teased out from Western Europe's annual personal consumption, which in 2008 exceeded that of the United States for the first time in history. Both the Western Europe economic region and the United States have personal consumption by their respective citizens in excess of 10 trillion USD.[20] The difference between them is that Europe has grown and in fact has nearly doubled since the start of the millennium on January 1, 2000, while the United States has increased by only a third. There are a variety of reasons why consumption has risen faster in Europe. Among them is the success of the euro, due to the reduction of internal frictions and costs as national currencies gave way to a unified regional currency.

People are better off in the Eurozone than they were a decade ago because of the strength and dependability of their currency. The long march of the euro to successful equilibrium with the U.S. dollar is complete. Perhaps euro dominance as the world's reserve currency is underway.

There was one event in the 10-year lifespan of the euro that interrupted this process. In late 2004, the U.S. Congress passed and the Bush administration accepted a change in federal tax law.[21] By that change, international companies headquartered in the United States were allowed a one-time repatriation of foreign accumulated profits at a particularly low tax rate. For one year only, the federal corporate income tax rate was about 5 percent instead of 35 percent. Companies seized the opportunity to bring foreign earnings back to the United States, and did so in an amount measured in the hundreds of billions of dollars.

The law required that the repatriation be done in U.S. dollars. That had two consequences. Companies abroad that did not hold dollars but had accumulated earnings over the years in their foreign subsidiaries needed to raise the dollars by either:

- Borrowing in euros or other currencies and converting to dollars.
- Accumulating the dollars by selling euros or other currencies. The repatriation itself had to be done in dollars.

Second, the statute required those companies to have a trail of the use of the dollars for a certain period of time. They could not use the dollars, for example, to pay dividends or executive compensation. The purposes for which dollars could be used were defined. Companies would face tax penalties if they violated the rules. Therefore, many businesses segregated the dollar payments into a dollar hoard so they could track it and demonstrate compliance with the law.

The 2004–2005 one-time event increased the demand for U.S. dollar balances. While all dollars were fungible in normal transactions, the risk of a tax penalty encouraged U.S. multinational companies to follow this hoarding technique as a precaution.

These tax code changes caused world businesses to buy dollars and sell foreign currencies, particularly the euro. We saw the dollar strengthen against the euro (see Figure 1.7). Once the repatriation period was over, the U.S. dollar resumed its weakness against the euro and has continued that trend through today.

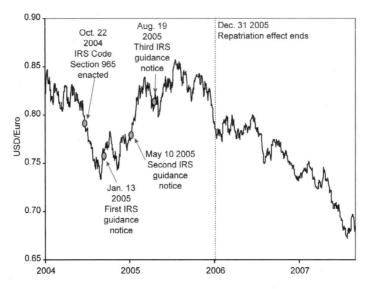

Figure 1.7   Effects of 2004–2005 Repatriation Tax Change, Data through July 2009
Source: Federal Reserve Bank and Cumberland Advisors.

Outlook for the Euro

The authors of this book expect the euro to strengthen over the next decade. As mentioned above, the political construct of the ECB has become increasingly credible during this past decade, while the Fed's credibility is seen as being undermined by the Obama administration's proposals. This comes on top of a fundamental problem in the United States, namely, the economy's lack of savings and reliance on foreign capital to finance investment, a long-term negative for the dollar.

Notwithstanding all of the political elements in Europe, which are complex and volatile, it is important to note that the Eurozone continues to enlarge. The financial crisis has taught non-Eurozone members and the European Union that it is better to be a part of the Eurozone than to go it alone.

If one looks at inflation rates, currency-exchange rates, and interest rates in the Eurozone countries versus non-Eurozone countries, one is continually reminded that the euro is the better option. Today, we see most of the remaining countries in the European

Union attempting to qualify and enter the Eurozone through the Exchange Rate Mechanism (ERM).

As this book is written, Baltic countries are attempting to accelerate their qualifications so that they can be admitted to the Eurozone. In other countries that are not qualified and in peripheral European countries that are not EU members, the euro is the dominant outside currency. No longer does the U.S. dollar play the number-one role. There is a de facto acceptance of the euro as a reserve currency and as a store of value. This is true even when there is no de jure compliance with the terms of the ERM.

Travel to Ukraine, which is not a member of the European Union, and you find the euro is widely accepted. The same is true in Turkey. Furthermore, in continents outside the European area, the euro has a stature that is now equal to or perhaps even ahead of the dollar's. The authors have seen that in both Africa and Asia.

To sum up, in only 10 years the Eurozone economy has grown larger than the U.S. economy. Euro-denominated cash in the world exceeds U.S. dollar cash. Euro-denominated international debt equals U.S. dollar-denominated international debt.

Last, and of special interest to readers of this book, euro-based stock-market shares of global market caps have been growing relative to dollar-based shares. If the trends in currency, economic size, and debt aggregates continue, stock-market weight must eventually follow.

CHAPTER

2

Convergence and Integration

It ain't over till it's over.

—Yogi Berra

Value preservation and growth are guiding principles of investment decisions. Depth of markets, liquidity, removal of inefficiencies, and lower transaction costs are parts of that equation and the
outcome of financial integration.

We saw these dynamics emerging in the 1990s, in part thanks to
the peace dividend, fiscal discipline, the IT revolution, and low inflation. In Europe the Maastricht Treaty forged an economic framework that led to a massive convergence of interest rates, the single
currency, and a single market for goods and services. In the United
States, President Clinton's 1993 budget act raised taxes, cut spending, and, along with the New Economy, brought a solid economic
expansion and budget surpluses.

The bursting of the tech bubble in 2000 and the terrorist attacks
on the United States changed this framework. The Bush administration accelerated fiscal spending and cut taxes massively, bringing
the federal budget back into deficits, while monetary policy remained
accommodative. In Europe, some erosion of fiscal discipline has
accompanied the early-decade slow-growth environment and the
European Union's (EU) enlargement.

Where do we stand today in the aftermath of the recent financial crisis? This chapter discusses the implications for investors of the relative positions of the EU, where fiscal slippage remains limited, and of the United States, where profligate debt issuance puts serious stress on the national savings rate.

The 1990s: A Virtuous Economic Framework in Europe and the United States

We review herewith the policy changes put in place in both Europe and the United States that led to solid economic growth during the 1990s, specifically, the making of the EU single market in Europe and the adoption of restrictive fiscal policies in the United States.

The March toward Market Integration in Europe[1]

A great shock generally coerces policymakers into policy reform and even vision. In Europe there has been no lack of such shocks. The concept of a European Union likely had its roots deep in Europe's twentieth-century traumatic history, as a prevention of the recurrence of war. The collapse of the Bretton Woods system was also a catalyst for the quest toward greater European economic stability and integration.

It was in 1979 that the nine member states of the European Economic Community agreed on the European Monetary System, which introduced the Exchange Rate Mechanism (ERM). The ERM fixed their currencies within an adjustable exchange-rate band. It would take another ten years for the blueprint of the Economic and Monetary Union (EMU) to emerge and for the European Union to be established and ratified by the Maastricht Treaty, on February 7, 1992.

The process was arduous although methodical, and truly extraordinary. The EMU went through three stages: First, the creation of a single European Market established between 1990 and 1993 the free movement of persons, capital, goods, and services. Second, between 1994 and 1998, the creation of the European Monetary Institute set the framework for the convergence of monetary and economic policies, leading to the introduction of a single currency. And third, January 1, 1999, saw the irrevocable fixing of exchange rates, the transfer of monetary-policy conduct to the ECB, and the introduction of the euro as the single currency. (The euro banknotes and coins as legal tender were introduced on January 1, 2002.)

The Maastricht Treaty required countries to achieve a high degree of convergence, based on specific criteria:

- A high degree of price stability
- Sound public finances
- Stable exchange rates
- Low and stable long-term interest rates
- Independent central banks

In May 1998, 11 of the 15 EU member states had met the criteria for the adoption of the single currency.[2]

Benefits of Market Integration in Europe

The single market profoundly transformed the EU's financial structure. Some of the obvious benefits emerged as a result of removing market inefficiencies and minimizing the asymmetry of information present in fragmented European equity and corporate bond markets.

The scope of benefits is of course considerably wider. We would cite several areas of positive change:

- The euro area became one of the largest economies in the world.[3]
- The single currency eliminated currency risk and volatility and has led to a single market of goods and services that is easily comparable across borders.
- The single monetary policy led to "harmonization" of rates; key central bank rates are set by the ECB and are the same for all the countries in the Eurozone.
- The legislative and legal framework sought to ensure a single set of rules pertaining to financial instruments and, thereby, equal access to markets,[4] while financial development reduced transaction costs,[5] and institutional investors enhanced cross-border equity-capital flows.[6]

The policy process that led to the single market, that of the pursuit of price stability and sound public finances, contributed to a significant decline in long-dated yield levels (see Figure 2.1).

More important, the new policy framework sparked a phenomenal convergence of long-dated yield levels among member states relative to the benchmark member, Germany. The spreads narrowed sharply (see Figures 2.2, 2.3, and 2.4), implying a dramatic

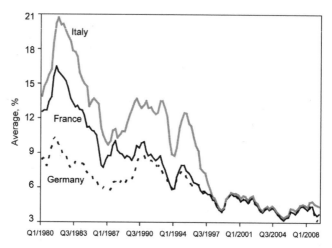

Figure 2.1   10-Year Benchmark Government Bond Yield (AVG, %), Q1/1980–Q2/2009
Source: Haver Analytics.

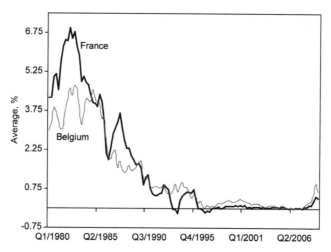

Figure 2.2   10-Year Government Bond Yield Spreads: France and Belgium Minus Germany (AVG, %) Q1/1980–Q2/2009
Source: Haver Analytics.

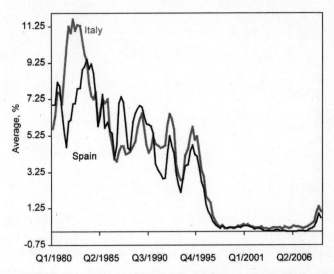

Figure 2.3   10-Year Government Bond Yield Spreads: Italy and Spain Minus Germany (AVG, %) Q1/1980–Q2/2009

Source: Haver Analytics.

Figure 2.4   10-Year Government Bond Yield Spreads: Greece Minus Germany (AVG, %) Q1/1992–Q2/2009

Source: Haver Analytics.

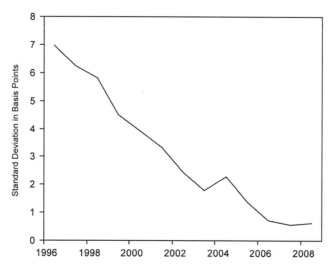

Figure 2.5   EU25-Convergence of Short-Term Interest Rates Annual Data (Standard Deviation, in bp)
Source: Eurostat.

decline in the relative cost of capital in these countries. (The orthodoxy of German policymaking in the pursuit of fiscal and price stability has made German markets the anchor.)

Quantitative indicators of financial integration, such as standard deviation (see Figure 2.5) and coefficient of variation (see Figure 2.6), also underscore the great degree of convergence of interest rates.[7] In the case of fully integrated bond markets, bond yields should only react to news common to all markets, so that a decline in the standard deviation and in the variation coefficient of interest rates should indicate an increasing degree of financial market integration.

In the United States

The combination of the peace dividend, the Clinton administration's ambitious program of tax increases, and spending cuts brought a drastic turnaround in the state of public finances. In 1998 the budget went from perennial deficits to a surplus, the first in two and a half decades (see Figure 2.7), and the debt-to-GDP ratio dropped from 49.4 percent in 1993 to 33 percent by 2001 (see Figure 2.8).

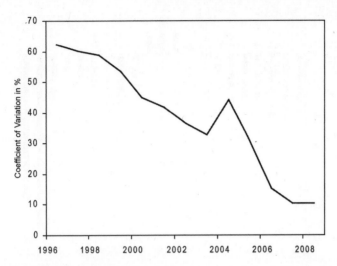

Figure 2.6 EU25-Convergence of Short-Term Interest Rates Annual Data (Coefficient of Variation, in %)
Note: The coefficient of variation of annual rates of EU and of Eurozone countries is defined as the ratio (in percentage) between the standard deviation of the rates and their average. It is a measure of the variability in rates between countries that takes into account the average level of the interest rates in question. For example, a spread of 1 percent between the interest rates of countries is considered by the indicator as a much lower variability during a year when the average level of rates is at 15 percent (range 14 to 16 percent) than for a year when the average level is 1.5 percent (range 0.5 to 2.5 percent). When the rates are identical, the indicator is zero. Giuliano Amerini, Interest rates: An overview. Eurostat: Economy and Finance 26 (2003).
Source: Eurostat.

These policies, along with perceived high-quality U.S. assets (benefiting from the institutional framework of the rule of law and strong corporate governance, accounting standards, and rating agencies) and liquid markets made the United States the market of choice for foreign investors. Foreign capital inflows surged (see Figure 2.9), setting the stage for the global trade imbalances that emerged in the latter part of the decade and into the current one.

The U.S. current account balance swung from a small surplus of close to 0.5 percent of GDP in 1991 to a yawning deficit of 4.5 percent of GDP in 2000, on its way to 6.5 percent just a few years later (see Figure 2.10).

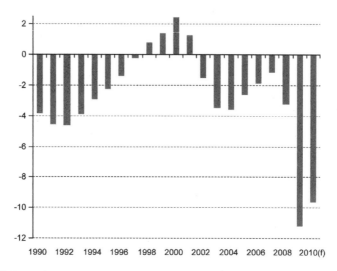

Figure 2.7   U.S. Budget Deficits (-)/Surpluses (+) as Percent of GDP, by Fiscal Year 1990-2010

Source: Congressional Budget Office.

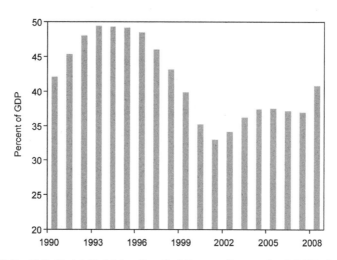

Figure 2.8   U.S. Debt Held by the Public, as Percent of GDP, by Fiscal Year 1990-2001

Source: Congressional Budget Office.

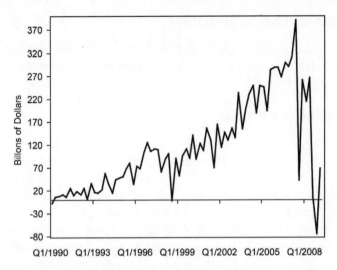

Figure 2.9   Net Foreign Purchases of U.S. Securities, Q1/1990–Q1/2009 in Billions of Dollars, Quarterly Data
Source: Haver Analytics.

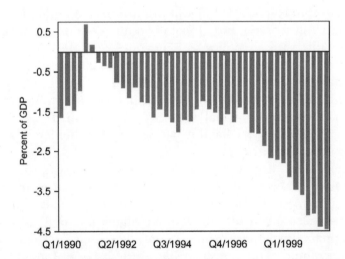

Figure 2.10   U.S. Current Account Balance, as Percent of GDP, Quarterly Data, Q1/1990–Q4/2000
Source: Haver Analytics.

The 2000s: Fiscal Slippage

In a climate of fiscal discipline erosion on both sides of the Atlantic, U.S. pro-growth policies contrast sharply with the more cautious euro area policies.

A Turnaround in U.S. Policies

As mentioned at the outset, the bursting of the tech bubble in 2000 and the terrorist attacks on the United States changed the virtuous policy framework of the 1990s. The Fed lowered rates aggressively, and the Bush administration cut taxes massively, while accelerating fiscal spending. By 2002, plusses turned back to minuses, and the budget balance swung from a $236-billion surplus in 2000 to a $377-billion deficit in 2003. The cumulative deterioration totaled a whopping $613 billion. In GDP terms, this represents 5.9 percentage points. About one-third of the deterioration reflected cyclical factors, that is, changes in the business cycle, and about two-thirds reflected legislative/structural factors, such as the tax cuts and additional spending.

The countercyclical U.S. fiscal impulse had tangible effects on both the United States and global economies, so that investors did not take this shift in policy as a negative and the United States remained the market of investors' choice. In 2002 and 2003, both defense and non-defense spending pulled more weight in GDP, the average tax burden had of course declined dramatically, and some rebalancing of the financial structure in favor of Treasuries and a less-leveraged private-liability structure had helped corporate balance sheets recover.[8]

By mid-2004, however, with global growth close to a thirty-year high, calls for the fiscal pendulum to swing toward restraint had gathered momentum, but the return to fiscal prudence did not actually materialize. Instead, the United States pursued a relatively expansionary fiscal policy in an economy that essentially had reached full employment. The paradigm had shifted: Large foreign capital inflows prevailed, even accelerated, providing cheap credit and fueling domestic demand growth and trade imbalances, without much concern about the impact on national savings. Hard deficit-cutting policy choices were postponed. At the same time, the strength of the dollar early in the decade was instrumental in keeping monetary policy more accommodative for longer.

Foreign capital flows are of two types. Foreign direct investment is the most stable form of financing, generally geared at longer-term investments in productive assets, and portfolio flows into bonds and stocks tend to be a more volatile form of financing the lack of savings in a country. Portfolio flows into bonds have dominated foreign capital inflows into the United States in the late 1990s/early 2000s. They reflect two major trends.[9] The first trend is flows from Asia that are tied to that region's export-led economic growth model. They mirror trade flows, and in the early part of the decade that growth model was well in place, thanks to the demand impulse from the tax-cut-driven U.S. consumer. Foreign-exchange intervention added to that dynamic, as intervention to prevent home currencies from appreciating against the dollar (in order to ensure ongoing exports to the United States) meant buying dollars and reinvesting them into U.S. Treasuries. That was the case of Japan's massive intervention in 2003.[10]

The second trend is flows from Europe, seeking yield and duration in a more liquid and diversified market. We have observed that changes in pension rules in Europe, which caused firms to scale down equity investments and match liabilities more closely with fixed-income investments, along with demand from insurance companies, helped this trend.[11]

As long as foreign investors expect the return on capital to be greater in the United States than elsewhere, capital inflows to the United States will be sustained.

Slow Growth in the EU

In contrast to U.S. pro-growth policies, euro area policies spelled caution. As discussed in Chapter 1, the introduction of the euro was accompanied by funds having moved temporarily out of national currencies into U.S. dollars, leading to an initial decline in its foreign exchange value. This added to the ECB's inflation concern. The ECB's other major inflation worries were the effects on price stability of a "rounding up" in retail prices at the time of the currency conversion and of the various food-price shocks. These factors kept monetary conditions relatively tight. On the fiscal side, euro-area policy was framed within the Stability Pact's target ratios of 3 percent deficit-to-GDP and 60 percent debt-to-GDP. Slow growth implied some fiscal slippage both in the cyclical and structural fiscal

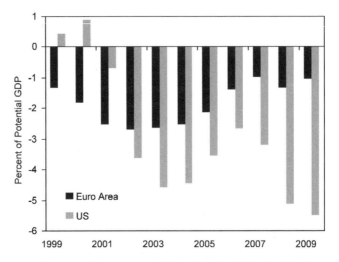

Figure 2.11 General Government Cyclically Adjusted Balances Surplus (+) or Deficit (-) as a Percent of Potential GDP
Source: OECD Economic Outlook 84 Database.

balances between 2000 and 2002, but, unlike in the United States, policies aimed at fiscal consolidation were put in place thereafter (see Figure 2.11).

The policy focus centered on the sustainability of social-security systems (pension and health-care reforms in particular) across Europe. Despite the mildly restrictive fiscal policies put in place in early 2003, meeting the Stability Pact's targets proved difficult. Regional differences also emerged. For example, France at the time had a slightly countercyclical fiscal policy, while Germany had adopted restrictive measures but registered a cyclically induced deterioration in its deficit. Italy adopted one-off measures, and Spain maintained its balanced budget.[12]

The 2008–2009 Financial Crisis: Europe as an Alternative to the United States

Time of reckoning: The crisis revealed the resilience of the EU financial integration and the fragility of U.S. financial institutions.

Strength of Euro Convergence

The degree of EU market integration achieved over the past decade has been truly remarkable. Ironically, it probably enhanced the contagion effect of the financial crisis between markets across the euro area and asset classes. The ECB reported a sharp drop in euro-area investment funds' holdings of equities, suggesting a combination of negative valuation effects, an erosion in the role of institutional investors as a conduit of funds relative to banks, and a strong "home bias" among investors, since a large part of the drop in equity investment was related to equity holdings issued outside the euro area. The financial crisis had an impact on bond markets as well, as seen in Figures 2.2 through 2.4. The sharp reduction in risk appetite and flight-to-quality flows led to a widening of long-dated yield spreads between euro-area sovereign bonds and German bunds. These events even led some investors to conjecture about the possible demise of the euro-area experience.

The recent thawing of financial markets set the stage for a partial reversal of the widening of spreads (see Figures 2.12 and 2.13). Money data for June 2009 indicates a rise in euro-area financial institutions' holdings of domestic assets, suggesting some thawing in credit conditions at banks. Importantly, the partial reversal of spreads implies that the structural factors of financial integration and convergence in the euro-area markets are prevailing.

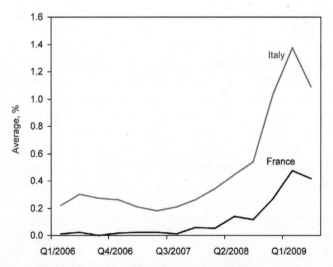

Figure 2.12   10-Year Government Bond Yield Spreads: France and Italy Minus Germany (AVG, %) Q1/2006–Q2/2009

Source: Haver Analytics.

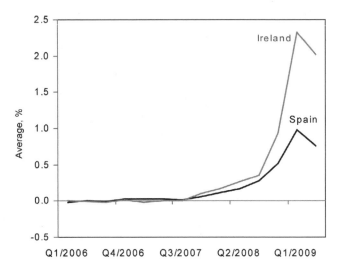

Figure 2.13   10-Year Government Bond Yield Spreads: Ireland and Spain Minus Germany (AVG, %) Q1/2006–Q2/2009
Source: Haver Analytics.

Challenges for the United States

The financial crisis unmasked serious excesses committed in the financial industry over the years and called into question both the perceived superiority of U.S. financial institutions and the sustainability of global imbalances. That said, the academic literature will continue to debate whether the U.S. current-account deficit reflects unsustainably low national saving or a comparative advantage in supplying high-quality assets.[13] What we do know, however, is that the dollar has weakened as foreign investors have demanded a price concession for their purchases of U.S. assets, but it also rallies whenever risk appetite drops. This suggests that the dollar's status as a reserve currency prevails and remains an important factor for international investors. Barclays Capital recently commented that "As long as the dollar's status as reserve currency is stable around current levels, other risk indicators (debt/GDP, contingent liabilities, etc.) would have to worsen to unrealistically high levels for the United States to experience a downgrade" of its triple-A sovereign rating.[14]

We would take a less sanguine view than Barclays. We believe that these "risk indicators" are real and will likely erode further the foreign-exchange value of the dollar and foreign investors' appetite

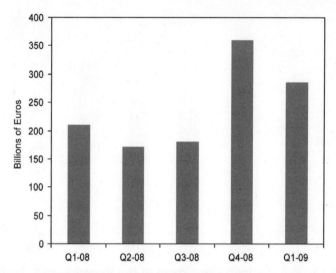

Figure 2.14   Net Portfolio Investment in the EU-27, Excluding FDI and Derivatives (Quarterly Data, in Billions of Euros)
Source: Eurostat.

for U.S. assets in favor of other regions, one being the EU. Illustratively, portfolio flows in the EU remained more stable than in the United States over the past five quarters and did not drop to the same extent as they did in the United States in Q1:09 (see Figures 2.14 and 2.15).

We also note that a recent survey conducted by the Division on Investment and Enterprise at the United Nations Conference on Trade and Development (UNCTAD) shows that there is an increased preference by multinationals to invest in emerging markets, Asia in particular. For the location of Foreign Direct Investment (FDI) in 2009 through 2011, the BRIC countries (Brazil, Russia, India, and China) dominate, while the EU has become an important competitor to North America as an FDI recipient.[15]

The past several decades witnessed:

1. In the EU, the emergence and development of a single market with a single currency, framed by a single monetary policy and a fiscal template that seeks discipline.
2. In the United States, a major turn from a virtuous monetary/ fiscal policy framework to fiscal profligacy.

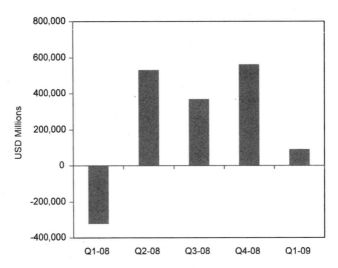

Figure 2.15 Net Portfolio Investment in the United States, Excluding FDI and Derivatives (Quarterly Data, in Millions of Dollars)
Source: U.S. Bureau of Economic Analysis.

The current financial crisis has not spared the two regions. Policy makers have been extremely proactive in their attempts to contain the crisis and restore financial stability, leaving investors with the key question: Which of the two regions has the most adequate policy framework and the institutional will to normalize policies while restoring asset quality? We believe the financial development and integration of the EU over the past 10 years have produced a financial environment that is a viable investment alternative to the United States.

3

Taxation

There is nothing new under the sun.

—Ecclesiastes 1:9

No book discussing stock market investments in the United States versus the Eurozone or European Union would be complete without a chapter on taxation. This book is no exception.

The approach to taxation has to be considered three ways:

1. What is the total tax burden on the economies in which one chooses to invest or to avoid investing?
2. How are taxes levied in the countries in which one will invest?
3. What is the taxation on the investment results when one makes those investments?

U.S. Federal Taxation

For an American, the U.S. government's taxation of investors is relatively straightforward. The federal government extends a long-term capital-gain status to investments made by U.S. investors, as long as the investment is held for more than one year. Investment profits derived from a holding period shorter than one year are taxed at ordinary income rates. Long-term capital-gain rates are considerably lower than ordinary income tax rates in the United States.

In 2009, long-term capital gains were taxed at a maximum rate of 15 percent and short-term gains at a maximum rate of 35 percent. Capital losses could be used to offset gains on a dollar-for-dollar basis under the federal tax code. In addition, the federal government allows unused losses to be carried forward against future gains. Three thousand dollars of unused losses can be charged annually against ordinary taxable income.

U.S. State Taxation

In addition to the federal government, there is significant taxation of capital gains by the states. Some states, like Wyoming and Florida, do not tax gains at all. Other states do. New Jersey, for example, levies an income tax on capital gains. The top tax bracket in New Jersey is 10.75 percent. Table 3.1 shows the ten highest state income tax rates in the United States. Because many states do not offer any special treatment for capital gains, this chart reflects the tax rate on capital profits as well. In addition, many states, such as New Jersey, do not allow taxpayers to carry forward a loss to a future year and use it to shelter the taxes on a gain. Thus, state tax policy is often in conflict and is counterproductive to federal tax policy.

U.S. taxation of investors has varied over time and can be enormously complex.[1] The Bush administration instituted the 15-percent

Table 3.1 Ten Highest Marginal Income Tax Rates

State	Top Rate (%)
Oregon	11.0
Hawaii	11.0
New Jersey	10.8
California	10.6
Rhode Island	9.9
Vermont	9.4
Iowa	9.0
New York	9.0
Minnesota	7.9
Idaho	7.8

Source: David Hale, "Has the U.S. Recession Ended?" *Global Economics 7* (July 31, 2009), 11.

long-term capital-gain tax, the lowest in the modern investor's memory. The Obama administration has indicated that this and other tax rates will rise substantially after the financial crisis has passed.

European Taxation

In Europe, taxation of investors is equally complex and varies greatly among countries.[2] A general distinguishing comment is that some countries treat capital gains at a flat rate while others treat them as ordinary income couched in a progressive tax structure. Illustratively, in Estonia, capital gains for individual investors are treated at the flat ordinary income rate of 21 percent, in Romania at the flat income rate of 16 percent, and in Belarus at the flat income rate of 12 percent. Hungary applies a 25 percent rate on individual capital gains, while the personal income tax structure is progressive, with the rate rising from 18 to 36 percent. In Spain, capital gains incurred by individuals are taxed at 18 percent, while the personal income tax rate rises from 24 to 43 percent. In France, capital gains from sales of securities are taxed at an 18 percent rate and those from property sales at a 16 percent rate, to which must be added a social security surcharge of 11 percent—but the top marginal rate is 45 percent.

The Netherlands treats capital gains for individuals as ordinary income, and the personal tax rate basically rises from 25 to 52 percent. Similarly, in Italy, capital gains are generally treated as ordinary income, with the personal income tax rate rising from 23 to 43 percent, while in Denmark the top marginal tax rate attains 59 percent. Belgium makes a distinction between capital gains on assets derived by individuals engaged in businesses, which are subject to the ordinary corporate income tax rate of 33 percent, and those derived by individuals not engaged in business activity, which are generally not taxed. In Germany, capital gains also tend to be treated as ordinary income, if it is a real estate asset held for fewer than 10 years or another type of asset held less than a year. The top marginal rate for individuals is 47.5 percent, including the 5.5 percent solidarity surcharge.

It is fair to say that the EU remains a high-taxation region for individuals. Total tax revenues, including social-security contributions, average slightly below 40 percent as a percentage of GDP for the EU-27. But the wide range in the top personal income tax rates, from 16 percent in Romania to 59 percent in Denmark, suggests that new member states tend to rely less on direct taxes and thus have lower tax rates than the EU as whole.

David Hale's July 31, 2009, commentary[3] identified the forthcoming tax risk associated with the Obama administration proposals. Hale wrote, "The Obama tax proposal will also create problems for state governments with high marginal tax rates. If his tax proposals are enacted, he would give five U.S. states the second highest tax rates in the world after Denmark (60 percent) and above Sweden (56.44 percent)."

Corporate Taxation

Let's now examine corporate taxation. Businesses that are headquartered in the United States and treated as American corporations are among the most highly taxed in the world. Figure 3.1 shows com-

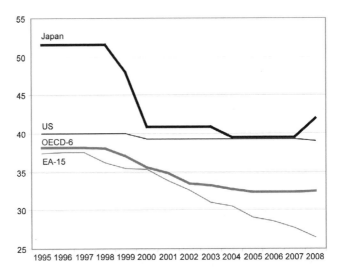

Figure 3.1   Comparative Corporate Tax Rates for OECD Countries (in Percent)

Source: *Taxation Trends in the European Union, Main Results.* European Commission Directorate-General for Taxation and Customs Union together with Eurostat, the Statistical Office of the European Communities. European Commission, Luxembourg: Office for Official Publications of the European Communities, 2008.

parative tax rates for OECD countries in Europe, Japan, and the United States. Only Japan has higher corporate tax rates than the United States. Various member states of the European Union have significantly lower rates than the United States.

In addition to the current high corporate taxation rates in the United States, it is expected that the Obama administration will extend and enlarge corporate taxation as part of its longer-term approach to U.S. tax policy. There are very few market players who expect corporate business taxes in the United States to decline. At best, they may remain constant but be altered by the abolition or adjustment of tax-code provisions that currently act to soften the tax rates. The demands to finance the huge deficits in the United States are expected to put continuous upward pressure on business and corporate tax rates as well as personal-investment tax rates.

Comparing Taxation by Region

Typically, taxes are broken down into four categories, according to the OECD. They are personal income taxation, corporate income taxation, taxes on social contributions, and taxes on goods and services. The total becomes the tax burden on the economy or region. The normal method of comparing taxation by regions or by large economies is to compute the total tax revenue as a percentage of the gross domestic product (GDP). Figure 3.2 shows the tax revenue ratio for the European Union and the United States, from the most recent data available at the time this book was written.

Looking superficially at tax burden only, the United States would seem to be a more favorable place to invest than the European Union. As with all other things, the devil is in the details. The key is to examine the component parts. The tax burden of the European Union is higher because of consumption taxes. Specifically, the biggest revenue raiser and the most important tax in the European Union is the value-added tax (VAT). The United States does not have a value-added tax and is now the only OECD country without one. Sales and consumption taxes are mostly levied at state and local levels in the United States.

In addition, the United States is engaged in a huge fiscal expansion. That means the federal government, according to estimates by the Congressional Budget Office, is financing in excess of one trillion dollars per year in the debt markets. So the debt/GDP ratio of

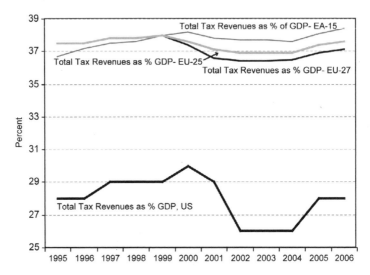

Figure 3.2   Total Tax Revenue Ratio for European Union and United States (as a Percentage of GDP)
Source: Eurostat; U.S. Bureau of Economic Analysis.

the United States is extraordinarily high and is expected to continue climbing.

Taxation Versus Debt Financing of Government

The concept of financing government through debt versus taxation is an interesting one and a subject of debate among economists and financial professionals. In the European Union we find a higher tax burden, which translates to higher tax revenues as a percent of GDP, in order to finance the spending decisions of the political organizations involved in the EU. In the United States we have large spending decisions only partially financed by taxation. The rest is done with borrowing.

A fundamental question may be clarified if we focus on the difference between financing government spending with borrowing versus taxation. If you use taxation, the government's fiscal policy is more in balance. Deficits are smaller because current revenues are used to pay for governmental expenditures. If you use borrowing, the region or country is engaged in deferring the taxation. During that initial phase, when borrowing is increasing, the citizens of the country can experience what has been called in America "a free lunch." This continues as long as the credit markets are able to absorb the additional government debt that is being issued.

That has been the case in the United States as it uses its status as the world's largest economy and largest reserve currency to facilitate this expansive fiscal initiative launched by the Obama administration. To be fair, the Bush administration expanded the deficits hugely prior to the financial crisis. The Obama administration has grown them even more. The ratio of annual newly issued debt in relation to GDP under Obama is increasing at double-digit rates.

The authors of this book believe that fiscal expansion has its limits. One cannot borrow perpetually and expansively without eventual consequences. The nature of the consequences can be higher taxation, reduced consumption, devaluation of the currency, or credit-market seizure, among the possible outcomes.

In any case, there will be consequences, and those consequences will certainly befall the United States at some point in the foreseeable future. The authors of this book contend that the U.S. debt being offered to the world is without precedent in peacetime history, both in total amount and as a proportion of GDP. It will alter the competitive nature of the United States.

The Shift from the United States to Europe

As the world realizes that fiscal-policy expansion has to be continuously refinanced and that the burden of it falls on U.S. businesses and investors, the world will reallocate away from the United States at an accelerating pace. It is this reallocation process that suggests that European stock markets and the European financial structure can outperform those of the United States.

Prior to this period of peacetime fiscal expansionism, one could argue that the less bureaucratic and more entrepreneurial structure of the United States, which favored freer markets and less government spending and intervention, was able to support the notion that U.S. stock markets and investments could command higher valuations than in Europe. Price-earnings ratios, price-book ratios, price-sales ratios, stability of earnings, global participation by U.S.

companies, and favorable tax treatments for foreign direct investments by U.S. companies in other countries and regions in the world all combined to give the United States a competitive edge.

In the past, we looked at the Europeans and saw a more social-democratic structure than in the United States, which resulted in narrower profit margins, lower productivity, and more government intervention. In the past, we looked at the United States as the contrary and more growth-oriented economy.

We believe that has changed. The United States is quickly gravitating toward a structure in which it has more social-democratic functions, ever-larger governmental interventions, more managed industrial policies coming from Washington, and higher taxation. When you add the debt-financed portion of the federal budget to the taxation-financed portion, the government's share of GDP now rivals that of the European Union.

We have noted in other chapters that in the currency realm, the euro-versus-dollar decision is now clearly in favor of the euro as a dominant, respected, and valued currency in the world. We can also note that the structure of taxation is becoming an equalizing force between the United States and the European Union. At the margin, that means global business will move toward the currency, region, and countries where taxation is more favorable, if all other things are equal. That is one of the reasons the authors of this book believe that the European economy and its stocks and stock markets will evolve to parity or even eventually exceed those of the United States. This tendency will accelerate as the Obama administration's deficit-financing policy continues to unfold.

There are details in the rates of taxation that point to continuous support for this point of view. Figure 3.3 shows the adjusted top statutory tax rate on corporate income in the European Union and the United States. Clearly, if you are a business and looking only at corporate income taxes as an expense of doing business in your selected country, you would favor one in the European Union over the United States.

Interestingly, there is a diversity of taxation among the countries within the European Union. Figure 3.4 depicts the top statutory rates on corporate income throughout the world. Within the European Union there is a second division, which is apparent. The original fifteen members of the European Union have higher tax rates than the twelve newer members.

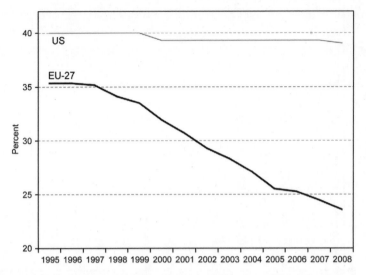

Figure 3.3   Top Statutory Rate on Corporate Income—European Union and United States (in Percent)
Source: *Taxation Trends in the European Union, Main Results.* European Commission Directorate-General for Taxation and Customs Union together with Eurostat, the Statistical Office of the European Communities. European Commission, Luxembourg: Office for Official Publications of the European Communities, 2008.

Corporate Taxation in Europe Is Shrinking

The reduction of taxation in Europe accelerated in the 1990s, after the Maastricht Treaty and the opening up of central Europe, as Russian domination receded and those emerging economies began to develop their own policies. Overall taxation, business taxation, and corporate taxation rates among the twelve new members of the European Union are lower than in the original fifteen. Baltic and central European countries have seized this opportunity, and businesses have relocated to them in order to benefit from this lower taxation while at the same time engaging a labor force that is well educated. This emerging central European membership in the European Union has put downward pressure on taxation in the original fifteen member countries, and that pressure has caused the entire structure of corporate taxation in Europe to shrink.

Tax policies tend to play a role in the choice of location of businesses and factories and in their ability to attract capital. A 2009

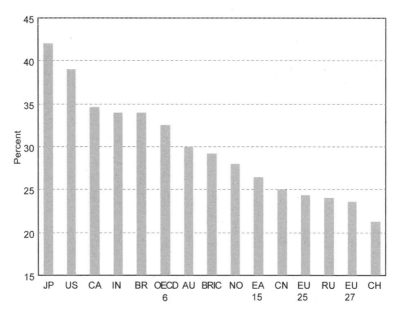

Figure 3.4   Top Statutory Rates on Corporate Income—World (in Percent, 2008)

Source: *Taxation Trends in the European Union, Main Results.* European Commission Directorate-General for Taxation and Customs Union together with Eurostat, the Statistical Office of the European Communities. European Commission, Luxembourg: Office for Official Publications of the European Communities, 2008.

OEDC analysis of taxation shows a "tax and growth ranking" of taxes, measuring their negative effect on GDP per capita. The study found changes in corporate taxes to be the most detrimental to growth, followed by personal income taxes, consumption taxes, and last by property taxes. The relative mobility of these factors plays an important differentiating role, according to the OECD.

Corporate income taxation is a factor in firms' investment decisions, and thereby in their production, job-creation, and innovation decisions. High statutory tax rates are one factor that reduces after-tax rates of return on investment, arguably a negative development for growth. But other factors, such as depreciation schedules, need to be taken into account as well to fully ascertain the cost firms incur in using capital (i.e., the user cost of capital).

In addition to investment decisions, corporate tax rates influence productivity. The OECD study cites five channels of influence:

1. High statutory corporate tax rates tend to affect the relative price of production, making capital more expensive than labor.
2. They can reduce firms' incentives to invest in innovative activities. Tax incentives for R&D expenditures would offset this negative effect.
3. They may discourage foreign direct investment. Inbound foreign direct investment increases productivity of national firms.
4. They may increase administrative costs.
5. They may affect corporate financing decisions, such as debt-over-equity financing.

This general framework has encouraged the newer EU member states to pursue very low corporate income tax rates.

The gap in statutory corporate tax rates between the EU and the United States continues to grow and is in favor of the EU. The above-cited factors, such as generous depreciation schedules, labor mobility, low labor costs, and a longer tradition of a wide disparity in taxation among states, have translated into a very low tax-adjusted user cost of capital in the United States. That was the United States' advantage over Europe. It is changing.

We believe that the economic crisis has brought important changes to the U.S. landscape that may lead to a rise in the U.S. user cost of capital relative to the EU. The explosion of U.S. government debt, the new and emerging regulatory framework, and the shift from a financing to a funding model are factors that will likely raise the cost of capital for U.S. firms. The lack of tradition in the United States of increased involvement of the government in the economy is another factor that will differentiate firms that are nimble enough to take advantage of a government-private partnership in key sectors from those that will see their competitiveness eroded. But significant tax differences, which favor Europe over the United States, will prove to be a powerful force.

4

Stock Market Evolution

The horse is here to stay, but the automobile is only a novelty—a fad.

—President of the Michigan Savings Bank, advising Horace Rackham (Henry Ford's lawyer) not to invest in the Ford Motor Company, 1903. Throwing caution to the winds, Rackham disregarded his banker's advice and bought $5,000 worth of stock. When he sold his shares several years later, they were worth $12.5 million.

When it comes to the evolution of stock exchanges, New York and, for that matter, the United States are really newcomers. The Dutch East India Company founded the first stock exchange in Amsterdam, Netherlands, in 1602. The Paris stock exchange disagrees and claims its origins date back to 1540, and the London stock exchange cites 1698 as its starting date. In any case, by the time Henry Hudson sailed up the river that now bears his name (he was an employee of the Dutch East India Company), stock exchanges in Europe were already well underway.

European exchanges have had their history of bubbles and manias, and several books have been written on the matter. *Extraordinary Popular Delusions and the Madness of Crowds,* by Charles Mackay, and *Manias, Panics and Crashes,* by Charles Kindleberger, serve as outstanding sources for discussions of manias and their histories.[1]

The New York Stock Exchange officially commenced in March 1817, when 24 stockbrokers decided to operate an exchange and set up their clearing arrangements, operating under the Buttonwood Agreement, which was named for the buttonwood tree on Wall Street where they used to meet and transact in ownership shares of early U.S. companies prior to 1817.

Fast-forward to the post-World War II period. The United States is the dominant financial and global power. The strength of the dollar and the depth of its world reserve status are well entrenched. The post-war New York capital market is developing into the deepest and largest in the world. The combination of equity trading, debt markets, and capital-raising activities is being consolidated in New York. The New York Stock Exchange is growing into the ranking exchange of the world. The American Stock Exchange and the over-the-counter market, subsequently consolidated into the NASDAQ, continue the evolution in the United States.

European Exchanges, Pre- and Post-Maastricht

In Europe, up until the time of the Maastricht Treaty in 1992, each of the 27 current member countries of the European Union had its own stock exchanges (see Figure 4.1). Each one cleared transactions in its own currency. Each had its own operating rules and its own ownership structure. In the case of former USSR–dominated countries, those stock exchanges didn't commence activity until the early 1990s.

Maastricht changed all that. The development of the euro as a currency facilitated the change. Stocks could now list in a consolidated exchange and trade in one currency under rules established by the European Union.

The initiation of cross-border stock trading had actually started in the 1970s in Europe and expanded as agreements among countries and various exchanges evolved. There is an extensive history of that development, which is beyond the scope of a single chapter of this book. For further discussion of details regarding the political developments leading to Europe's modern stock exchanges, readers may wish to consult *The Origins of Europe's New Stock Markets,* by Elliot Posner.[2]

Original Name	Sept. 2009 Stock Exchanges	City	Country	Started	Ended
Athens Exchange	Athens Exchange	Athens	Greece	1876	current
BME Spanish Exchanges	BME Spanish Exchanges	Madrid	Spain	1800s	current
Borsa di Commercio	Borsa Italiana SpA (London SE Grp)	Milan	Italy	1808	2007
Bratislava Stock Exchange	Bratislava Stock Exchange	Bratislava	Slovakia	1991	current
Bucharest Stock Exchange	Bucharest Stock Exchange	Bucharest	Romania	1882	current
Hungarian Stock Exchange	Budapest Stock Exchange Ltd.	Budapest	Hungary	1864	current
Bulgarian Stock Exchange - Sofia	Bulgarian Stock Exchange - Sofia	Sophia	Bulgaria	1914	current
Cyprus Stock Exchange	Cyprus Stock Exchange	Nicosia	Cyprus	1996	current
Frankfurt Stock Exchange	Deutsche Börse AG	Frankfurt	Germany	1625	current
Irish Stock Exchange	Irish Stock Exchange	Dublin	Ireland	1793	current
Ljubljana Stock Exchange	Ljubljana Stock Exchange	Ljubljana	Slovenia	1924	current
London Stock Exchange	London Stock Exchange	London	England	1698	current
Luxembourg Stock Exchange	Luxembourg Stock Exchange	Luxembourg	Luxembourg	1927	current
Malta Stock Exchange	Malta Stock Exchange	Malta	Malta	1992	current
Copenhagen Stock Exchange	NASDAQ OMX - Copenhagen	Copenhagen	Denmark	1996	2005
Helsinki Stock Exchange	NASDAQ OMX - Helsinki	Helsinki	Finland	1912	2003
Riga Stock Exchange	NASDAQ OMX - Riga	Riga	Latvia	1993	2003
Stockholm Stock Exchange	NASDAQ OMX - Stockholm	Stockholm	Sweden	1863	1998
Tallinn Stock Exchange	NASDAQ OMX - Tallinn	Tallinn	Estonia	1991	2003
National Stock Exchange of Lithuania	NASDAQ OMX - Vilnius	Vilnius	Lithuania	1993	2004
Amsterdam Stock Exchange	NYSE Euronext - Amsterdam	Amsterdam	Netherlands	1602	2000
Brussels Stock Exchange	NYSE Euronext - Brussels	Brussels	Belgium	1801	2000
Bolsa de Valores de Lisboa e Porto	NYSE Euronext - Lisbon	Lisbon	Portugal	1769	2002
Paris Bourse	NYSE Euronext - Paris	Paris	France	1540	2000
Prague Stock Exchange	Prague Stock Exchange	Prague	Czech Republic	1993	current
Warsaw Stock Exchange	Warsaw Stock Exchange	Warsaw	Poland	1817	current
Wiener Börse AG	Wiener Börse AG	Vienna	Austria	1771	current

Figure 4.1 Eurozone Stock Exchanges

Note: The Spanish Stock Exchange, or BME, which stands for Bolas y Mercados Espanoles, is a collaboration of the various stock exchanges that deal with the systems and the securities that are traded within Spain. Under the umbrella of the BME Group are the following: Iberclear Stock Exchange, Valencia Stock Exchange, BME Consulting, Barcelona Stock Exchange, Madrid Stock Exchange, and Bilbao Stock Exchange.

Source: World Federation of Exchanges

One of the significant characteristics of the development of the new European exchanges was the opening of exchanges in smaller countries. Innovative enterprises could now find capital more easily than under the antiquated rules that existed after World War II. Maastricht greatly advanced the entire process. As the euro developed as a currency, as the European Union continued to flourish, and as stock-trading rules continued to consolidate, so did stock exchanges. One by one national exchanges became merger partners with either Euronext or OMX. By the summer of 2009, the 27 separate national exchanges had consolidated into 19.

The larger the stock exchange, the more cross-border activity; the more cross-border activity, the larger the quotations systems that would clear electronically in a common currency. The larger the quotations systems, the faster the stock markets evolved. The results of the ongoing consolidation of stock exchanges can be shown in the number of companies now trading in Europe, versus those trading on U.S. exchanges.

At the time of the launching of the euro and during Maastricht's implementation, there were more companies trading on the three U.S. exchanges than in all of the European exchanges combined (see Figure 4.2). By August 2009, the number of companies trading on European exchanges had nearly doubled, while the number of companies on U.S. exchanges had fallen by more than 25 percent.

Detractors blame this change, in which European stock markets have expanded much more rapidly than those in the United States, on a number of issues. Some critics suggest it's the result of the Sarbanes-Oxley reporting requirement, which imposes liabilities that can be avoided if companies list on European exchanges. To some extent this is true; however, there are other factors that also support the development of stock markets in Europe at an expanding and intensifying pace relative to the United States.

In Chapter 2, we discuss how financial markets improve their pricing and their efficiencies. These benefits to asset-market pricing should not be underestimated when it comes to equity prices. As markets evolve, they get more scrutiny and they are better understood. They deepen in terms of liquidity and, therefore, entice entrepreneurs to use them as a platform for raising capital. Furthermore, the establishment of those markets and the currency that supports them adds to their credibility, and in a circular fashion one improvement begets another.

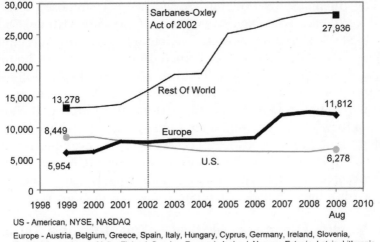

US - American, NYSE, NASDAQ

Europe - Austria, Belgium, Greece, Spain, Italy, Hungary, Cyprus, Germany, Ireland, Slovenia, England, Luxembourg, Malta, Finland, Sweden, Denmark, Iceland, Norway, Estonia, Latvia, Lithuania, France, Netherlands, Portugal, Poland, Turkey, Switzerland

ROW - Includes 32 exchanges in South America, Canada, Africa, the Middle East, Asia, and the Pacific.

Figure 4.2   Total Number of Listed Companies—1998 through August 2009
Source: World Federation of Exchanges.

The expansion of the European Union from 15 to 25 and subsequently to 27 countries added Central Europe and emerging-market components to the overall stock exchange system of Europe. In the beginning, the stock exchanges of the fifteen countries of "Old Europe" had cross-border investments in the newer members. For example, the companies listed on the Austrian Stock Exchange had substantial investments and activity in the new Central European 10-country membership. Austrian trades were denominated in euros. Investors sought positions in such stocks in order to participate in the growth of Central Europe as it emerged from years of Soviet domination.[3]

Early stock-market mergers during the 10 years following the establishment of the euro as an active currency were centered in the original 15 member countries. Later, mergers expanded into the newer additions. In fact, some occurred before the countries themselves joined the European Union. Latvia, for example, merged into OMX in 2003, and Lithuania in 2004. The stock-exchange combination in the Baltics actually preceded the admission of those countries to the EU.

The financial crisis of the last several years imposed tests on these European stock exchanges, just as it did in the United States. The U.S. stock market peaked in October 2007; the subsequent decline in stock prices was exacerbated by the failure of Lehman Brothers in September 2008. The rest of the world was following more or less the same timetable and experienced similar results. After the failure of Lehman Brothers, stock prices around the world fell in a highly correlated manner. One would expect this, if global financial integration had been successful. In fact, ample proof of financial integration can be found in the correlated way in which the markets around the world trade. This is particularly true of the relationship between European and American stock markets.

U.S. Versus European Markets—The Balance Shifts

The left pie in Figure 4.3 shows the percentage of European stocks as compared to the United States and the rest of the world in 1998, at the launching of the euro. The weights in August 2009 are depicted in the pie on the right. It is evident that the European exchanges achieved higher proportionate growth in value than U.S. exchanges

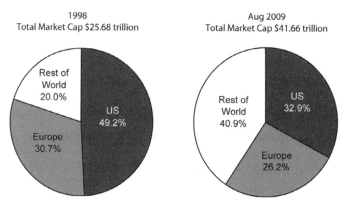

1998
Total Market Cap $25.68 trillion

Rest of World 20.0%
US 49.2%
Europe 30.7%

Aug 2009
Total Market Cap $41.66 trillion

Rest of World 40.9%
US 32.9%
Europe 26.2%

US - American, NYSE, NASDAQ

Europe - Austria, Belgium, Greece, Spain, Italy, Hungary, Cyprus, Germany, Ireland, Slovenia, England, Luxembourg, Malta, Finland, Sweden, Denmark, Iceland, Norway, Estonia, Latvia, Lithuania, France, Netherlands, Portugal, Poland, Turkey, Switzerland

ROW - Includes 32 exchanges in South America, Canada, Africa, the Middle East, Asia, and the Pacific.

Figure 4.3   Domestic Market Cap in USD—Year End 1998 and August 2009

Source: World Federation of Exchanges.

over the course of the 10 years. Not only are there more stocks trading in Europe than in the United States by almost two to one, but the market-value percentage of those companies is higher than it was 10 years ago, compared to the U.S. position. On December 31, 1998, the U.S. stock market was valued at \$12.65 trillion, out of a total of \$25.68 trillion for the world. In August 2009 the U.S. stock market was valued at \$13.69 trillion, out of a world total of \$41.66 trillion, while in Europe the total was \$7.89 trillion at the end of 1998 and \$10.9 trillion in August 2009.

The dominance of the United States and its stock exchanges peaked in the 1990s. At the end of 1998, after the Asian currency crisis, the Russian ruble problems, and the collapse of the Long Term Capital Management hedge fund, the U.S. stock markets comprised nearly half of the total value of the world's tradable equities. By August 2009 that number had declined to 33 percent. By comparison, on January 1, 1999, the total market value of all the European exchanges constituted 30.7 percent of the world. By August 2009 that percentage had decreased to 26.2 percent. The American and European declines are largely due to the dramatic increase in value in Asia. Asian growth has driven the rest-of-the-world component from 20 percent in 1998 to 40 percent in 2009. But the smaller decline of Europe compared to the United States is due to the strengthening of the euro and to the development of the European stock exchanges, which are growing at a faster pace and with greater financial integration than in the United States. The weakness of the United States is pronounced and dramatic: U.S. stock market shares went from half of the world to a third during this decade.

European Outperformance

Where does this lead us? It is the contention of the authors of this book that European stock markets will outperform the U.S. stock markets in a strategic way over the next several years. A variety of reasons are put forth to support this notion, including the ongoing successful convergence and financial integration of the European Union and the monetary policies of the European Central Bank of the Eurozone, compared with those of the Federal Reserve. The evolution of stock exchanges and their consolidation is a facilitating piece of this equation.

In fact, the authors believe that the time is soon approaching when companies in Europe and the United States will trade in a global exchange setting. Such transactions are already occurring. The merger of exchanges between the New York Stock Exchange and Euronext, for example, is taking us in the direction of global trading. The interaction of global capital markets can only benefit the smaller and growing ones at the expense of the larger and more mature ones. We would expect the trend that favors Europe over the U.S. to continue for this reason.

Through the guiding work of Vincenzo Sciarretta, the authors of this book have examined in other chapters the tools by which stock traders can determine which companies will outperform. There is considerable evidence that the tools work the same way in Europe as they do in the United States. Application of those tools and selection criteria may guide investors in successful stock picking.

The use of exchange-traded funds (ETFs) is discussed in detail in Chapter 5, for those Americans who seek investments in Europe using the ETF approach rather than the selection of individual stocks. Remember, ETFs are only baskets of the underlying individual companies. If the individual companies do not perform well, neither will the ETF. If the individual companies that collectively are in a region, in a country, in a currency, or in a sector do well, the ETF will reflect it in price.

In sum, stock markets have had a long but fragmented history in Europe, but now they are rapidly coalescing and strengthening there. In the United States, a more mature, consolidated market has already absorbed its regional exchanges and gone through the machinations of rapid growth and subsequent failure, when bubbles collapsed, and is now losing market share globally to other stock markets of the world, including the enlarging one in Europe.

CHAPTER 5

Accessing Europe with ETFs

The wisest mind has something yet to learn.

—George Santayana

This book lays out an argument for the outperformance of European equity markets over their U.S. peers. But an investor who examines, digests, and agrees with this argument has only fought half the battle. As always in investing, it's not enough to know *where* to invest; you must also know *how* to make that investment.

Investors looking to Europe must answer a series of critical questions. This chapter lays out those questions, reviews the data surrounding each argument, and ultimately explains why, for most investors, low-cost exchange-traded funds (ETFs) represent an important option. From there, we examine 23 Europe-focused equity ETFs, along with a variety of internationally focused sector ETFs. The goal is to provide you with the tools you need to pinpoint the right funds for a given portfolio.

Stocks or Funds?

The first and most immediate question an investor must answer is whether to purchase individual stocks or broader, more diversified mutual funds. Other chapters in this book will focus on the stock-investing alternative. This one is for the ETF investor.

Investors with less than $1 million to invest may decide not to consider individual equities. It is impossible to build a reasonably diversified portfolio without a substantial amount to invest. Investing in just a handful of international stocks can be risky. While the themes identified in this book suggest there is a tailwind for European equities, there is no airtight guarantee that any single stock or company will perform well. Management might be crooked or incompetent; the company could make a poor strategic choice; any number of things could go wrong.

Micro-Efficient, Macro-Inefficient

Stock markets are micro-efficient. On the level of individual securities, it's very difficult for an individual investor to have an informational advantage over the market.

Ten or 20 years ago, you might have had a shot. But the advent of the Internet and new regulations requiring fair disclosure of market-moving information to all participants has made it much more difficult to gain an advantage. There is simply too much information available today and too many investors working to profit from it.

To invest in individual stocks, you must believe that you know more about HSBC, Vestas, or Nestle (or whatever company you choose) than highly paid analysts working at hedge funds, securities analysts at leading investment banks, retired corporate officers, journalists, and the rest of the world. This fly in the stock-picker's ointment is doubly true for U.S. investors looking abroad. They do not have the same boots-on-the-ground feeling for certain companies that local investors enjoy.

None of that means that investors should abandon hope and simply pursue a naïve global indexing strategy. A strong case can be made that, while markets are efficient on a *micro* level, they are inefficient on a *macro* level. Evidence suggests (and recent market bubbles confirm) that investors often misread major trends in the global economy, either overlooking valuable assets or investing with eyes closed into the jaws of a market-distorting bubble.

Compared to individual securities, the rules on the macro level leave room for informational advantages. There are no regulations, for example, requiring full and fair disclosure of market-moving economic data, government policy, or demographic information. Similarly, the ranks of competent analysts who consider these trends are far smaller than the football stadiums full of single-securities analysts. The reason for this is simple: Investment banks have historically funded single-security analysts as a way of soft-selling their investment-banking services. Macroeconomic analysis has no such product base. So while a firm may employ over a hundred individual-securities analysts all over the world, its core macroeconomic and asset-allocation team can (and likely does) fit into a small meeting room once a week.

As a result, we believe that one of the opportunities for U.S. investors to outperform lies in capitalizing on big-picture inefficiencies, rather than company-specific insights. And exchange-traded funds, not single securities, are the easiest and most efficient way to do that.

Active or Passive?

If an investor decides to use a mutual fund to access Europe, rather than hand-selecting individual equities, the next question becomes: active or passive management?

An actively managed mutual fund will employ a team of professional stock analysts to do exactly the kind of individual-company analysis mentioned earlier. These analysts try to pick stocks that will outperform their benchmarks.

They enjoy a number of advantages over the lay investor, beginning with the fact that it is their full-time job to evaluate and understand the companies they cover.

By contrast, an index fund will simply try to track an index. In the United States, investors are quite familiar with index funds tied to benchmarks like the S&P 500 or the Russell 2000 indexes. Similar funds exist tracking European indexes, including broad-market indexes, individual-country indexes, and in some cases individual-sector indexes.

Active management has an intuitive appeal. After all, who wants to settle for average returns when you could do better?

Unfortunately, the data show that the likelihood of actually beating the market with an active fund is very low. Standard and Poor's has a running analytical series that compares the returns of actively managed funds against their passive benchmarks over time. The data is uniformly unfriendly for active managers. For the five years stretching from 2004 to 2008, for instance, the S&P 500 outperformed 71.95 percent of actively managed large-cap mutual funds in the United States. The S&P SmallCap 600 outperformed 85.5 percent of small-cap funds.[1]

The focus of this book is on Europe, and while S&P doesn't have a standalone European category, it does look closely at the performance of international funds. The story here is the same. For the five years ending in 2008, 83.5 percent of international mutual funds trailed the relevant benchmark (the S&P 700). Small-cap active managers did better, but even here a majority (58.8 percent) trailed their benchmark (the S&P Developed Ex-US SmallCap Index).[2]

Why do so many managers fall short? The answer, originally advanced by Jack Bogle, the founder of the world's first retail index fund, is simple: Cost matters.

Because index funds only aim to track their benchmarks, they are easier and therefore cheaper for fund companies to run. These savings are often passed along to shareholders in the form of lower expense ratios.

As Nobel Prize winner William F. Sharpe has pointed out,[3] investors—as a class and by definition—own the entire market. Therefore, you can expect the average investor (and therefore the average mutual fund) to trail the market by the amount of its fees. Because actively managed mutual funds cost more to run than passive index funds, the average actively managed fund will underperform its index peer.

Can You Pick a "Good" Active Manager?

Many efforts have been made to identify ways to predict manager performance, without much success.

The Morningstar mutual-fund ratings service, to take one example, has not been shown to have any real long-term predictive power regarding mutual fund performance. As the old saying goes, past performance is no guarantee of future success: Just ask investors who owned shares in Bill Miller's Legg Mason Value Fund. After beating the market in each of 15 straight calendar years, the Legg Mason Value Fund suffered such a terrible performance blow in 2008 that its 10-year return dipped below the market average. It's extraordinarily difficult to sort the good managers from the bad ahead of time.

And it may be unnecessary.

Studies show that a vast majority of an investor's risk and returns are tied, not to individual-manager or security selection, but to asset allocation choices. Investors looking to add alpha to their portfolios should focus on getting the right mix of assets, overweighting individual regions, countries, or sectors based on their understanding of the evolving economic environment. They should leave the fool's gold of stock picking (and active fund picking) to others.

Mutual Fund or ETF?

Investors who have gotten this far are left mostly with good choices. Investors who focus on low-cost index mutual funds will guarantee themselves the market's return, less a small amount of fees. That's a fine start.

To maximize returns, however, a few questions remain, the most important of which may be: mutual fund or exchange-traded fund?

It's a question that's only become important over the past five years, as ETFs have emerged as a legitimate alternative to traditional mutual funds. For investors with substantial portfolios, the choice between ETFs and mutual funds can have a major impact on long-term after-tax returns.

What Is an ETF?

First, let's start with the basics: What is an ETF? The answer is simple: An ETF is a special kind of mutual fund.

Much of the mainstream media misses this point, but ETFs operate under the same regulatory structures and generally provide the same types of exposures that mutual funds do. Just as an S&P 500 index mutual fund will track the S&P 500 by holding all 500 securities in the index, so too will an S&P 500 ETF. An investor who buys shares in a mutual fund buys a pro-rata stake in the securities it holds; the same rule applies for the ETF.

How do they differ? ETFs offer three key advantages compared to traditional mutual funds, as well as one major drawback.

Intraday Liquidity

The first key advantage that ETFs offer is hinted at in the name: *exchange-traded* fund. At its core, an ETF is a mutual fund that is traded on an exchange.

In a traditional mutual fund, buy and sell orders are processed once per day; for U.S. investors, after the close of trading on the New York Stock Exchange. If you decide to buy a mutual fund at, say, 10 a.m., your order to purchase shares will not be processed until 4 p.m. In the interim, the market could rise, fall, or stay flat; you are at its mercy.

An ETF, by contrast, is exchange-traded: You can buy and sell it just like a stock. If you decide to buy an ETF at 10 a.m., you can submit a market order at 10 a.m. and take the fill. If you change your mind later in the day, you can then sell it. Your profit or loss would vary depending on where the market moved in the interim.

In fact, you could buy an ETF at 10:00 a.m., sell it at 11:15 a.m., and then buy it back again at 3:32 p.m. Often, you can even buy and sell options on an ETF. An ETF, in short, functions just like a stock, bought and sold from the comfort of a regular brokerage account with the same ease as buying shares of IBM or JPMorgan.

For internationally focused funds, this intraday liquidity provides an extra advantage. The European market is closed during much of the U.S. market day. As a result, the underlying securities held by most European mutual funds or ETFs do not actually trade during U.S. market hours. Typically, the price at which you buy or sell a traditional mutual fund will reflect the price at which the underlying securities closed earlier in the day; new information will take a further 24 hours to process.

This creates a problem, because the global markets are often serially correlated. That is, what happens in the U.S. market influences the markets in Asia, and what happens in Asia influences the markets in Europe, and so on as you move around the globe. This means investors can wait to see how the U.S. market performs before they place buy and sell orders for European mutual funds. Savvy investors can often buy in for less than "fair market value" in the fund. This sounds great if you're buying, but it slowly erodes the value of the holdings of long-term shareholders in the fund—there's no free lunch.

With an ETF, the feedback from the open market is immediate and this market distortion minimal. Because there is a live market in the ETF during U.S. market hours, investors will drive the price of the ETF either up or down based on their expectations for where the price of the underlying European securities will open tomorrow. In a very real way, it's like an extended European trading day during

U.S. market hours. Although this presents a few challenges when buying and selling ETFs—something we'll discuss briefly at the end of this chapter—intraday liquidity is nonetheless a significant advantage for U.S. investors.

Lower Costs

Exchange-traded liquidity is directly linked to the second key benefit ETFs offer: lower costs.

When you buy shares in a traditional mutual fund, you send a check directly to the fund company. It issues shares based on the closing value of the fund's holdings at the end of the day. The fund company must process your order and keep records of how many shares you hold; it must send you prospectuses and statements; it must include you in its family of shareholders. It also has to sit on your cash until the next market open and then purchase the securities it needs in a hurry to stay fully invested.

With an ETF, the process works differently. When you buy shares of an ETF, you simply buy them on an exchange from another investor who wants to sell. It works just like buying shares of IBM.

The result is that the fund company never needs to know. It doesn't have to keep records, send full prospectuses, or manage statements. All of that work is handled by the brokerage firm, just as it is with single stocks.

Further, when new money comes into an ETF, a large investor simply hands the ETF provider the full basket of stocks it needs to operate, and new shares of the ETF are issued with no transaction costs. These are called creation units.

As a result, it's easier and cheaper for a fund company to run an ETF than it is to run a mutual fund. Fortunately, most companies pass these savings on to shareholders in the way of lower expense ratios, with the result that index-based ETFs are often the lowest cost tools available for accessing the market. The Vanguard Total Market ETF (NYSE: VTI), for instance, provides exposure to virtually all the stocks in the U.S. equity market and charges just 0.09 percent in annual expenses. You can gain exposure to the entire international stock market for less than 0.30 percent. By contrast, the average asset-weighted expense ratio for a mutual fund in 2008 was 0.99 percent, according to the Investment Company Institute.[4] That difference in costs flows directly to an investor's bottom line.

Better Tax Efficiency

The final major advantage that ETFs offer over traditional mutual funds for U.S. investors is tax efficiency. Because of their unique structure, ETFs are far less likely to pay out capital gains distributions than traditional mutual funds. In 2008, for instance, Barclays Global Investors—the largest ETF provider—paid out gains on just two of its 178 ETFs in the United States.[5]

The *why* of this is a bit complicated, but goes to the heart of what makes an ETF an ETF, so it merits analysis.

As mentioned earlier, when an individual investor buys or sells an ETF, he or she interacts solely with other investors. The obvious question is this: What if everyone wants to buy an ETF and no one wants to sell (or vice versa)? Won't the share price go straight up, so that the value of the ETF is higher than the value of its underlying holdings? That's what happens in closed-end funds, a much-maligned cousin of ETFs.

ETFs differ from closed-end funds because of a unique arbitrage mechanism called the "creation/redemption process." It is this process that helps keep the ETF share price close to the value of its underlying holdings and also contributes to the funds' remarkable tax efficiency.

The process works like this: Imagine that investors become enamored of U.S. small-cap stocks. They flood into the market, specifically into the iShares Russell 2000 ETF (NYSE: IWM), one of the most popular small-cap ETFs on the market today.

As a result, IWM's share price begins to trade above the value of its underlying holdings. When this happens, a special type of institutional investor called an authorized participant, or AP, swoops in and "creates" new shares of the ETF to meet the need. They do this by buying up the underlying 2000 stocks in the index and delivering them to the ETF sponsor. In exchange, they receive an equal value in shares of the ETF, priced at the fund's true fair-market value.

The AP then sells those shares into the public market at the inflated price and captures the arbitrage profit. The act of flooding the market with new shares helps drive the price of the ETF back in line with its actual underlying value.

The process works the same in reverse. If the price of an ETF drops below the value of its underlying holdings, APs buy up shares of the ETF and trade them into the ETF company. In exchange, the

ETF company gives that AP the full value of the ETF paid out in shares of the underlying holdings. The AP can then go into the public market and sell those holdings, notching a profit. Meanwhile, buying pressure on the ETF helps drive its share price back in line with its underlying value.

This "creation/redemption" process not only reduces transaction costs for the ETF (further bolstering the lower-fees argument outlined above) but is the key to the tax efficiency ETFs enjoy compared to traditional mutual funds.

If you redeem shares of a mutual fund, the fund company must sell some of the securities it owns to raise cash to pay you. If the securities it owns have appreciated, the fund will realize a taxable gain. By law, that gain must eventually be distributed to ongoing shareholders in the fund.

In an ETF, the fund company almost never has to sell its underlying holdings. When an AP redeems shares, the ETF issue simply pays them "in-kind," as discussed earlier. In addition, the ETF issuer can select share lots with low tax bases to use during redemptions, so it can constantly rid itself of potential tax risks.

ETFs aren't perfectly tax efficient; there have been occasions when ETFs have paid capital gains distributions, particularly in non-core asset classes such as commodities or currencies, or in exotic ETFs like leveraged and inverse funds. Even plain-vanilla equity ETFs sometimes incur capital gains when they are forced to adjust to changes in the underlying index. But the record shows that the vast majority of plain-vanilla equity and bond ETFs rarely if ever pay capital gains distributions. They are as close as you can get to perfect tax efficiency in the mutual fund world.

Why Wouldn't You Buy ETFs?

If ETFs are generally cheaper, more liquid, and more tax-efficient than mutual funds, why doesn't everyone use them? Why hasn't the mutual fund business simply evaporated?

Well, there are a few tricky bits. For one, because ETFs are bought and sold like stocks, they are subject to the same commissions as stock trades. An investor with a limited amount of capital to invest, or who is dollar cost averaging on a quarterly or monthly basis, may find that the commissions quickly erase any cost savings from lower expense ratios or better tax efficiency.

In addition, like every stock on every exchange, there is always a small difference between what you can buy an ETF for and what you can sell it for. For most ETFs this spread is quite small, often a penny or two, but it's not zero. Investors should pay attention to these spreads and focus only on ETFs that trade well.

There are also some tricks involved in trading ETFs that can discourage inexperienced investors. For instance, despite the effective arbitrage system, ETFs often trade slightly above or slightly below their net asset value. For some investors, this difference may not be enough to matter. But for investors putting significant sums of money to work, a 0.25 to 0.5 percent swing in a fund's pricing can have a large dollar impact.

Investors can avoid most liquidity and pricing problems by focusing on ETFs with at least $50 million in assets under management, which screens out the more inefficient ETFs. Investors should also always use limit orders when trading, to limit the likelihood of receiving a "bad fill."

ETFs aren't the perfect choice for all investors, but given their low expenses, intraday liquidity, and tax advantages, they are a great choice for many.

ETF Choices for the European Market

Now that we have settled on ETFs, we come to the fun part: choosing the right ETF for the job.

It's not as easy as it looks. There are currently more than 760 ETFs available in the U.S. market.[6] According to IndexUniverse.com, a leading provider of data and analysis of ETFs, there are 11 ETFs focused broadly on Europe and the Eurozone, 12 ETFs focused on individual countries within Europe, and many more with significant exposure to European equities. Which fund you choose depends on your specific view of the equity marketplace and where exactly you want to gain exposure.

Buy the World

The first, and most basic, approach to gaining European exposure is simply to buy a global-equity ETF. The IndexUniverse.com ETF database captures six such funds, the most popular of which is the iShares MSCI All Country World Index ETF (NYSE: ACWI).

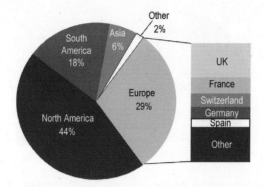

Figure 5.1 The Neutral Position: MSCI All Country World Index
Source: IndexUniverse.com and Bespoke Investment Group. Data as of June 30, 2009.

ACWI tracks an index whose stated goal is to be an equity benchmark for global stock performance. It holds securities located in both the United States and abroad, including both developed and emerging markets. As of June 30, 2009, the fund had $432 million in assets, and charged 0.35 percent in annual expenses.

Given its broad target, a fund like ACWI is clearly not the best way to target European exposure. But it does at least set the table for a benchmark exposure. The market-cap-weighted fund is 28.7 percent invested in Europe, defined broadly, holding securities in 19 different countries. The largest European weights are in the UK (8.8 percent), France (4.0 percent), Switzerland (3.5 percent), Germany (3.3 percent), and Spain (1.9 percent) (see Figure 5.1).

This should be considered a baseline. If you have 28.7 percent of your equity portfolio invested in Europe, you're taking a neutral position on its growth. If you're bullish, you should hold more than that.

Developed Markets

Many investors prefer to separate their international allocations from their domestic exposures. Rather than buying a single global fund, they will buy separate domestic and international equity funds, in different weights.

By far the most common means of gaining international exposure is through the MSCI EAFE (Europe, Australasia, and the Far

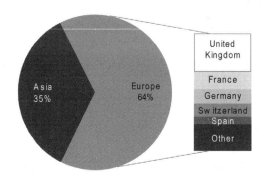

Figure 5.2   The Common Route: Europe in MSCI EAFE
Source: IndexUniverse.com and Bespoke Investment Group. Data as of June 30, 2009.

East) Index, which dominates the international index market the way the S&P 500 and Dow Jones Industrial Average dominate the U.S. market.

Two ETFs track the MSCI EAFE Index: the iShares MSCI EAFE Index (NYSE: EFA) and Vanguard Europe-Pacific ETF (NYSE: VEA). Together, they hold nearly $40 billion in assets.

The MSCI EAFE Index is designed to provide broad coverage of developed markets outside of the United States. The index is heavily weighted toward Europe, with 64.2 percent of the portfolio divided among 18 different European countries. The largest weights are in the UK (20.9 percent), France (9.8 percent), Germany (7.7 percent), Switzerland (7.4 percent), and Spain (4.5 percent). The remainder of the portfolio is focused on Asia, where Japan (24.0 percent) and Australia (7.4 percent) make up the bulk of the holdings (see Figure 5.2).

Emerging Markets

Many investors also sprinkle their portfolios with exposure to emerging markets. By far the most commonly used benchmark here is the MSCI Emerging Markets Index. The market-cap-weighted index is designed to provide exposure to 25 different countries around the world.

There are two ETFs offering exposure to the MSCI Emerging Markets Index: the iShares MSCI Emerging Markets Index Fund (NYSE: EEM) and the Vanguard Emerging Markets ETF (NYSE: VWO). Together, they have more than $50 billion in assets.

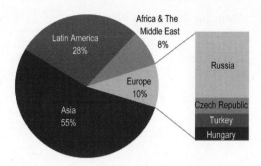

Figure 5.3   Not Much Room for Europe: MSCI Emerging Markets
Source: IndexUniverse.com and Bespoke Investment Group. Data as of June 30, 2009.

For investors looking to Europe for emerging-market exposure, however, the ETFs don't offer much. As of June 30, 2009, less than 10 percent of the portfolio was invested in European equities, with the bulk of that in borderline Russia (5.8 percent). The other exposures were the Czech Republic (1.5 percent), Turkey (1.2 percent), and Hungary (1.1 percent) (see Figure 5.3).

Europe-Specific ETFs

Fortunately, ETFs allow for much more specificity than the broader indexes provide. There are 23 ETFs focused specifically on European exposure, including nine broad-market ETFs, one small-cap fund, one emerging-markets fund, and 12 individual-country funds. The number continues to grow, so by the time this book goes to press it may be closer to 30.

Europe and the Eurozone

There are six ETFs offering broadly diversified exposure to European equities, and two additional funds focused exclusively on the European Economic and Monetary Union, providing investors with an array of choices on how to approach the market.

By far the largest and most popular Europe-focused ETFs are the iShares S&P Euro 350 (NYSE: IEV) and the Vanguard European Stock ETF (NYSE: VGK). The former had $1.6 billion in assets under management as of August 14, 2009, while the latter is part of a fund complex with more than $10 billion in assets under management.

Table 5.1   Broad-Market European ETFs

Fund	Ticker	Expense Ratio	AUM	Largest Country (Weight)	Largest Sector (Weight)	2008 Performance
BLDRS Europe 100 ADR	ADRU	0.30%	$18.7m	UK (38.9%)	Financials (23.7%)	−44.42%
iShares S&P Euro-350	IEV	0.60%	$1,600m	UK (32.8%)	Financials (22.7%)	−43.33%
PowerShares FTSE Europe	PEF	0.75%	$6.7m	UK (28.2%)	Financials (41.1%)	−48.73%
SPDR DJ STOXX 50	FEU	0.29%	$52.3m	UK (33.1%)	Financials (28.8%)	−42.45%
Vanguard Euro Stock	VGK	0.18%	$10,100m	UK (32.2%)	Financials (22.3%)	−44.85%
Wisdom Tree Europe Total Dividend	DEB	0.48%	$293.7m	UK (25.2%)	Financials (19.7%)	−42.60%

Source: IndexUniverse.com and Bespoke Investment Group. Data as of June 30, 2009.

Both IEV and VGK follow classic, market-cap-weighted indexes. As Table 5.1 suggests, they capture similar portfolios—note that the largest country and sector weights are nearly identical. They also delivered remarkably similar returns in 2008.

VGK is the cheapest European ETF available, charging just 0.18 percent and is a good foundational choice for most investors. Both funds, however, trade with tight spreads and will track the European market well, making them solid choices overall.

Figure 5.4 shows the country breakdown of IEV, although VGK's is similar. This should be considered the "base case" for the country breakdown of Europe as a whole.

An alternate approach is offered by the SPDR DJ STOXX 50 ETF (NYSE: FEU), which provides low-cost exposure to Europe with a fee of just 0.29 percent. The fund tracks the DJ STOXX 50 Index, an index holding 50 of the largest corporate giants in Europe. A U.S. investor might consider this akin to the Dow Jones Industrial Average of Europe.

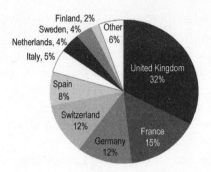

Figure 5.4   IEV: An Example of Market-Cap-Weighted Europe
Source: IndexUniverse.com and Bespoke Investment Group. Data as of June 30, 2009.

Because Europe is home to a number of banking giants, this fund's concentrated portfolio has significant exposure to the financial sector. As of June 30, 2009, FEU was 29 percent invested in financials, compared to 23 percent for VGK and IEV.

This is an important point: As you move away from broadly diversified market exposure and toward narrower indexes, you often create sector tilts.

Another example of this is found in the BLDRS Europe 100 ADR ETF (NYSE: ADRU), which holds the 100 largest European companies with listed American Depository Receipts trading in the United States. Many investors believe that ADR-focused ETFs have slightly better liquidity than ETFs holding internationally listed equities, since the shares that the ETFs hold trade at the same time and according to the same rules as the ETF itself. The downside, however, is that the market can be skewed by the fact that it only holds ADRs: Not every company goes through the effort to list its shares overseas, so you can gain a somewhat distorted view of the market. In the table below, for instance, the UK weighting for ADRU is more than 6 percent higher than its market-cap-weighted peers. That's because UK-listed stocks tend to list ADRs at a higher rate than continental firms. Given this distortion, and the limited assets under management, ADRU may not be the best choice for investors.

That leaves two additional funds, the PowerShares FTSE RAFI Europe (NYSE: PEF) and the WisdomTree Europe Total Dividend (NYSE: DEB). These two funds are distinct in that they follow what are called "fundamentally weighted indexes."

Fundamentally weighted indexes are indexes that use fundamental factors, such as dividends or sales, to determine how to weight each stock within an index, in distinction to traditional market-cap-weighted indexes, which link the weight of the company to its market value. Proponents of fundamental indexing argue that market-cap weighting leads indexes to overweight overvalued companies and underweight undervalued companies, creating a long-term performance drag.

One challenge with fundamental weighting systems is that they can create strong sector biases. As shown in Table 5.1, PEF is heavily invested in financials, with more than 40 percent of the portfolio focused on financial names. This high weight caused PEF to underperform in 2008 as financial companies came under pressure. (Note: PEF is a tiny fund, with just $6 million in assets under management.)

By contrast, DEB was one of the better-performing European ETFs in 2008, thanks in part to the low weight it assigned to financial firms. The fund pared back aggressively on its financials exposure as those companies cut dividends in 2008.

Eurozone

Investors who wish to focus exclusively on the European Economic and Monetary Union have two options: the SPDR DJ Euro 50 (NYSE: FEZ) and the iShares EMU Index Fund (NYSE: EZU). These funds exclude the UK, which, as shown in Table 5.1, represents more than 30 percent of the market capitalization of broader Europe.

Without the UK, both of these funds concentrate their portfolios in five countries: France, Germany, Spain, Italy, and the Netherlands. In the more diversified EZU, these five countries make up 88.0 percent of the portfolio; in FEZ, they account for 95.4 percent of the portfolio.

The difference between FEZ and EZU (see Table 5.2) is akin to the difference between FEU and VGK/IEV. The former in each case track narrow indexes composed of leading mega-caps and multinationals, while the latter offer broadly diversified exposure that stretches across market caps and regions.

Figure 5.5 shows how the exclusion of the UK alters the country breakdown of an EMU-focused ETF, using EZU as a proxy for the group.

Table 5.2   European Monetary and Economic Union ETFs

Fund	Ticker	Expense Ratio	AUM	Largest Country (Weight)	Largest Sector (Weight)	2008 Performance
SPDR DJ Euro 50	FEZ	0.29%	$303.7m	France (34.7%)	Financials (32.0%)	–42.90%
iShares EMU (Eurozone)	EZU	0.52%	$707.3m	France (30.4%)	Financials (25.0%)	–45.82%

Source: IndexUniverse.com and Bespoke Investment Group. Data as of June 30, 2009.

Dividend-Focused Europe

High-yield, dividend-focused investing has become a popular approach, and there is one ETF that takes a high-yield approach to the European market.

The First Trust Dow Jones STOXX European Select Dividend ETF (NYSE: FDD) invests in 30 of the highest-yielding components of the Dow Jones STOXX 600 Index, a broadly diversified European equity index. The actual methodology is somewhat complicated, but it focuses on firms that are paying high dividends, have a history of growing those dividends, and have sufficient earnings to cover those dividends in the future.

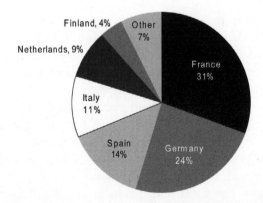

Figure 5.5   EZU: An Example of Market-Cap-Weighted Eurozone
Source: IndexUniverse.com and Bespoke Investment Group. Data as of June 30, 2009.

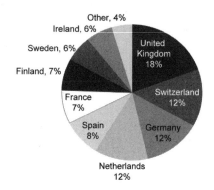

Figure 5.6   FDD: Dividend-Focused Europe

Source: IndexUniverse.com and Bespoke Investment Group. Data as of June 30, 2009.

As of June 30, 2009, the fund was well diversified across 13 European countries (see Figure 5.6), although its country weights varied significantly from a market-cap portfolio. Its largest weights were in the UK (17.8 percent), Switzerland (12.5 percent), and Germany (12.4 percent). The fund charges 0.60 percent in annual expenses and tends to be concentrated in financials, industrials, and utilities.

With just $6 million in assets under management, FDD is too small and illiquid for most investors.

Small-Cap Europe

Investors looking to move down the capitalization spectrum in Europe have only one choice: the WisdomTree Europe Small Cap Dividend Fund (NYSE: DFE). DFE holds the shares of small, dividend-paying companies and weights those companies in line with their total cash-dividend payout.

As of June 30, 2009, the fund was heavily concentrated in the UK (39.9 percent of the portfolio), with high weights in Italy (11.1 percent) and Sweden (11.1 percent). Compared to a traditional, European market-cap-weighted portfolio, CFE was strongly underweight Switzerland, Germany, and France.

Interestingly, the fund had the highest industrials weighting of any European ETF included in this study (32.5 percent). Compared to its peers, it was significantly underweight financials and energy.

As of August 14, 2009, it was paying a 30-day SEC yield of 4.83 percent, compared to a 1.12 percent yield on the broad-market IEV fund. DFE component companies had an average market capitalization of just $655 million, compared to more than $40 billion for IEV.

Unfortunately, this small-cap tilt hurt performance in 2008 and 2009: The fund substantially underperformed its larger-cap peers for the year ending June 30, 2009.

Still, the focus on yield may be attractive as a way of weeding out illegitimate small-cap firms from the mix. If you're interested in small-cap Europe, this is your only choice.

Note that the fund had less than $20 million in assets as of June 30, 2009. That's a bit too small for comfort: It means both that the fund may be illiquid and also that it stands some chance of closing down. But for now it remains the only European small-cap fund available in the ETF space.

Emerging Europe: GUR

Investors looking to invest broadly in "the new Europe" can do so using the SPDRs S&P Emerging Europe ETF (NYSE: GUR) from State Street Global Advisors. The fund, which charges 0.59 percent in annual expenses, tracks the performance of the S&P European Emerging BMI Capped Index, a float-adjusted index of publicly traded companies in emerging Europe.

As of June 30, 2009, the fund was heavily concentrated in Russia (61.4 percent), with the remaining exposure scattered among Turkey (15.3 percent), Poland (11.5 percent), Czech Republic (6.0 percent), Hungary (5.4 percent), and "other" (see Figure 5.7).

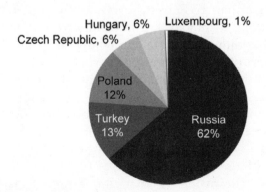

Figure 5.7 GUR: Emerging Europe
Source: IndexUniverse.com and Bespoke Investment Group. Data as of June 30, 2009.

The fund was focused in the energy (45.7 percent), financials (21.0 percent), and materials (10.7 percent) sectors. Note that GUR has more than four times the energy weighting of the broad, developed-market IEV.

The fund had $100 million in assets as of June 30, 2009, and inflows continued throughout the summer.

Single-Country

Investors wishing to drill down further can choose from a variety of single-country funds. With one exception, these funds are all issued under the iShares brand. The iShares ETFs are linked to MSCI indexes, which invest in locally listed companies and focus on the large- and mid-cap space. The only holdout—the Market Vectors Russia ETF (NYSE: RSX) from Van Eck Global—tracks the DAXglobal® Russia+ Index and holds a portfolio of 35 Russian companies listed either in Russia or on major global exchanges.

Most of the single-country funds charge just 0.52 percent in annual expenses. The exceptions are the Russia and Turkey ETFs, which charge 0.62 and 0.63 percent, respectively.

For the average investor, all of these single-country funds have sufficient liquidity to support reasonable investments, with each fund having more than $50 million in assets under management. Table 5.3 lists the funds and countries with single ETF exposure.

The obvious advantage of using single-country funds is that investors can fine-tune their allocations based on their exact preferences within the European area. An investor could take a major stake in the German ETF, using EWG, and completely ignore the United Kingdom, if that's what he wished to do. Or he could use the funds in conjunction with one of the broader ETFs outlined earlier, as a way of overweighting his favored markets.

The downside is that increasing the number of ETFs used increases the costs and complications of trading those ETFs. Remember, unlike mutual funds, investors must pay spreads and commissions each time they buy or sell an ETF. Managing a full European portfolio using single-country ETFs can be complicated for all but the largest accounts.

The other downside is that the coverage is incomplete. Missing from the list is all of Eastern Europe, as well as smaller Western European countries such as Portugal, Denmark, and

Table 5.3   European Single-Country ETFs

Country	Fund	Ticker	ER	AUM
Austria	iShares MSCI Austria Investable Market Index Fund	EWO	0.52%	$100m
Belgium	iShares MSCI Belgium Investable Market Index Fund	EWK	0.52%	$61m
France	iShares MSCI France Index Fund	EWQ	0.52%	$134m
Germany	iShares MSCI Germany Index Fund	EWG	0.52%	$442m
Italy	iShares MSCI Italy Index Fund	EWI	0.52%	$78m
Netherlands	iShares Netherlands Investable Market Index Fund	EWN	0.52%	$91m
Russia	Market Vectors Russia	RSX	0.62%	$727m
Spain	iShares MSCI Spain Index Fund	EWP	0.52%	$186m
Sweden	iShares MSCI Sweden Index Fund	EWD	0.52%	$128m
Switzerland	iShares MSCI Switzerland Index Fund	EWL	0.52%	$222m
Turkey	iShares MSCI Turkey Investable Market Index Fund	TUR	0.63%	$143m
United Kingdom	iShares MSCI UK Index Fund	EWU	0.52%	$642m

Source: IndexUniverse.com and Bespoke Investment Group. Data as of June 30, 2009.

Ireland. Given the pace of innovation, however, one might expect that to change soon.

Most important, given the integration of the European economy, the country-specific factors within Europe may be overwhelmed by the enormous differences in sector distributions across the various country funds. Consider, for instance, the differences in financials exposure across the various country funds (see Figure 5.8).

From 12 percent on the low side in Russia to 48 percent on the high side in Turkey, the differences are sharp. Each country's weight in this critical sector had a huge impact on returns over the past few years.

Financials aren't the only sector that matters, however. Especially for smaller ETFs, the differences can be stark. The Belgium ETF, for instance, is 38.0 percent exposed to consumer staples, while the German fund had just a 3.2 percent exposure as of June 30, 2009.

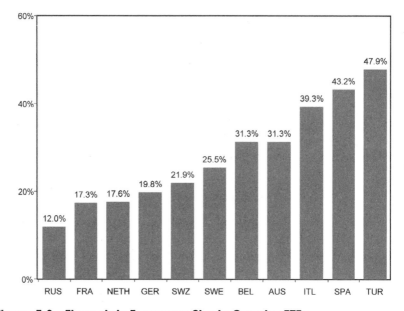

Figure 5.8   Financials Exposure: Single-Country ETFs
Source: IndexUniverse.com and Bespoke Investment Group. Data as of June 30, 2009.

Investors looking to use single-country ETFs must consider not just the national economy and economic policies, but the specific focus of publicly traded companies that happen to be headquartered (or listed) in each individual country.

Sector Exposure

Given the dominant role sectors play in driving stock market returns, many investors prefer to approach the market directly through sector-focused ETFs.

Unfortunately, there is as yet no complete family of Europe-focused sector ETFs on the market. There are, however, two complete families of internationally focused sector ETFs:

- SPDR S&P International Sectors
- WisdomTree International Sectors

The SPDR funds, from State Street Global Advisors, track sector slices of the S&P Developed EX-US BMI Index, a market-cap-weighted index of companies located in developed markets outside of the United States. This is the "standard" exposure, akin to buying the S&P 500 or its constituent sectors in the United States. The funds charge 0.50 percent in annual expenses.

The WisdomTree funds charge a slightly higher expense ratio of 0.58 percent, but compensate for that by paying higher average yields. The funds follow the WisdomTree dividend-weighting model mentioned earlier, which assigns higher weights to companies that pay larger total cash dividends. Like the SSgA funds, the WisdomTree products include companies from developed markets outside the United States.

One common criticism of dividend-weighting methodologies is that they skew the sector exposures of broad market indexes; i.e., a total Europe dividend-weighted index will have strongly different sector weights than a classic market-cap-weighted Europe index. That concern disappears, of course, when you focus exclusively on sectors to begin with.

The dividend tilt, however, does influence the balance between European and "other" (primarily Asian) exposure, as does the fact that S&P's index includes Canada (thereby lowering the European weights for the SSgA ETFs). By contrast, the WisdomTree products exclude both the United States and Canada. The end result is that the WisdomTree ETFs get the edge in terms of European exposure (see Table 5.4).

Unfortunately, few of these funds—either the SPDRs or WisdomTree products—trade in large volumes yet. They may have enough liquidity to support investment from smaller investors, but larger investors should approach the market carefully.

Real Estate

There is one narrow-focus ETF that homes in exclusively on Europe: the iShares FTSE EPRA/NAREIT Developed Europe Index Fund (NASDAQ: IFEU).

IFEU holds a concentrated portfolio of less than 100 companies that are "engaged in the ownership and development of the European real estate market," according to iShares. As of June 30, 2009, it was heavily focused on the UK (37.5 percent), France (28.3 percent), and the Netherlands (10.6 percent). The fund charges just 0.48 percent in annual expenses. Unfortunately, it hasn't caught on with investors, and as of August 14, 2009, had only $5.6 million in assets under management.

Table 5.4   International Sector ETFs: European Weights Compared

International Basic Materials		
SPDR S&P International Materials	IRV	45.7%
WisdomTree International Basic Materials	DBN	63.7%
International Consumer Goods		
SPDR S&P International Consumer Discretionary	IPD	50.9%
WisdomTree International Consumer Cyclicals	DPC	57.3%
International Consumer Staples		
SPDR S&P International Consumer Staples	IPS	73.7%
WisdomTree International Consumer Non-Cyclicals	DPN	81.3%
International Energy		
SPDR S&P International Energy	IPW	58.2%
WisdomTree International Energy	DKA	76.1%
International Financials		
SPDR S&P International Financial	IPF	55.1%
WisdomTree International Financial	DRF	63.4%
International Health Care		
SPDR S&P International Health Care	IRY	75.7%
WisdomTree International Health Care	DBR	68.6%
International Industrials		
SPDR S&P International Industrial	IPN	55.1%
WisdomTree International Industrials	DDI	65.3%
International Technology		
SPDR S&P International Technology	IPK	33.9%
WisdomTree International Technology	DBT	48.0%
International Telecom		
SPDR S&P International Telecom	IST	76.3%
WisdomTree International Communications	DGG	64.8%
International Utilities		
SPDR S&P International Utilities	IPU	71.0%
WisdomTree International Utilities	DBU	78.9%

Source: IndexUniverse.com, State Street Global Advisors, and WisdomTree Investments. Data as of June 30, 2009.

Approaching the Market with ETFs

The market for European-focused ETFs is diverse and growing. Investors can target Europe using ETFs in a variety of ways, including with global funds, international funds, broad-market European funds, single-country funds, or even sector proxies. The ideas expressed in this book are directly actionable using ETFs.

For investors who decide to enter this market, a few reminders are in order. When investing in ETFs, you must consider not just the cost of the fund's expense ratio but also the trading costs when entering and exiting a fund. Investors should focus mainly on established ETFs, looking carefully and skeptically at any product with less than $50 million in assets under management. We recommend that investors always trade using limit orders. Remember to look under the hood of ETFs to pinpoint the exact fund you want and the exact exposure you need.

This chapter by definition only touches on the differences among these funds and offers a static snapshot of the products as of mid-summer 2009. Fortunately, none of the information listed in this chapter is hidden from view. It's publicly available, often directly from the websites of the ETF providers themselves, where it will be updated in or near real time. Investors are advised to check that information before they make their decisions.

ETFs aren't right for everyone. But they are among the lower-cost, more tax-efficient ways to enter the market. And the choices for Europe and elsewhere are getting better each day.

PART

II

STOCK-SPECIFIC STRATEGIES

CHAPTER 6

Successful Strategies in the Eurozone

... to find some universal formula for it.

—Walter Pater

This chapter is all about backtesting of popular strategies in the Eurozone equity market. It tries to address basic questions, such as: Does the purchase of low price-to-book stocks make any sense? Is dividend yield a source of outperformance? Which indicators deserve respect? What happens if we combine a few factors to assemble a superb portfolio?

In fact, every stock investor tries to disengage the rewarding strategies from the mediocre, to separate the purest gems—call them the market-beating equities—from the dross, to find some universal formula for it. And with the emergence of fast computers and gigantic databases, many authors have backtested popular strategies to see whether they actually work, whether they are sound or just a charade.

As far as the U.S. stock market is concerned, the reader can find studies documenting 20, 30, 40, or more years of backtesting when searching for investment answers.[1] They generally agree that some characteristics are relevant to increase a portfolio's returns. Low price-to-sales stocks have fared well in the past. High dividend yields were a plus for large-capitalization companies. Low price-to-earnings stocks have shown contradictory results, but high price-to-earnings items were dangerous.

In the Eurozone, stock indexes are young and hence complete databases (with earnings, dividends, book values, and so on) generally offer a short lifespan, covering ten years or so. You may argue that such a short period is insufficient to reach reasonable conclusions. But if the conclusions are in line with what other authors have found for the United States in the long run, this reinforces the conclusions. In fact, European and American stocks breathe a common air and respond to the same dynamics. Why should the relative strength in a company's fundamentals play a radically different role on the two sides of the Atlantic? We did not see any valid reason. We thought, for instance, that if stocks with low price-to-book ratios were associated with an above-average performance in the United States, the same could be expected for the Eurozone. Our testing period tended to confirm that assumption.

A Short List of Good Ideas to Beat the Market

The following paragraphs report on tests of a number of popular investment strategies to see what works and what does not work well in the Eurozone. Generally speaking, the achievements are consistent with what other authors have found to be valid in the United States. The reader will discover that:

- Buying low enterprise-value-to-sales stocks is the best way to build an outperforming portfolio based on a single multiple.
- Low price-to-earnings stocks tend to beat the market, but only to a limited extent.
- Yes, dividends pay.
- A high return-on-equity ratio is the pet of many successful investors, yet taken alone it proved to be fruitless.
- Stocks with current market momentum may not have run out of steam.
- By selecting a combination of factors instead of a single one, you can turbocharge your portfolio.

What We Did

All the tests in this chapter use the FactSet Global Estimates database from December 31, 1998, through December 31, 2008. This 10-year period refers to the Dow Jones EURO STOXX Index, a basket of about 320 companies listed in the Eurozone. When the authors started the research, they asked Massimiliano Malandra to design and perform the tests. Malandra is a computer and balance-sheet expert with over 15 years of experience as a financial journalist in Italy.

The portfolios start with a €100,000 bet in a basket of 10 stocks, sharing an underlying feature (for example, the 10 stocks with the lowest price-to-book ratio or with the strongest return on equity in our universe). We then wait for a three-year period as the strategy "works." At that point, the portfolio is rebalanced and the results unfold over the next three years. The process repeats until the full 10-year period is covered.

To be even more clear: On December 31, 1998, we hypothetically invest €100,000 in the 10 stocks with, for instance, the lowest price-to-earnings ratio in our universe of equities. The basket runs until December 31, 2001 (that is, for three years). Then we rebalance the portfolio with the 10 new stocks showing the lowest price-to-earnings ratio and record their performance until December 31, 2004. The rebalancing act is repeated again to bring the portfolio up to December 31, 2007, when the final reshuffling occurs.

Cumulative results are then tallied and compared against the benchmark of the overall stock market. As the reader may have noted, the final time interval is just one year, from December 31, 2007 to December 31, 2008. This enables us to single out and evaluate performance during the Credit Crunch of 2008, one of the most brutal and ferocious periods in the history of financial markets. You may also ask why the portfolios are rebalanced every three years. There is no other argument than common sense here. We thought that three years was a good lifespan over which to let a fundamentals-driven strategy weave its magic. However, the tests were also conducted by reshuffling the portfolios every year instead of every three years; and the authors did not observe any particularly significant differences in the performance, so we stayed with the original three-year span.

Data: The Raw Material

Investment decisions can be based on historical data (like balance-sheets or earnings) or on forecast data (like consensus earnings estimates) or on a mix of both. Accordingly, Malandra ran the tests keeping in mind both approaches. In this chapter, when the portfolios are constructed on historical data, it means they refer to the latest annual figures officially reported by the company. To illustrate, if the portfolio is assembled on December 31, 2001, the data usually pertains to the 2000 balance sheet. While the time lag may seem excessive, it is in line with what most readers should be doing when building their own portfolios based on annually reported figures.

On the other hand, if the basket of stocks is based on forecast data, this refers to the latest annual data still to be reported by the company. To remain with our example, if we are building a portfolio on December 31, 2001, a company's forecast data are those for 2001, which is usually presented in March of the following year; and therefore the data represent a December 31 forecast. The consensus forecast data are the ones gathered by FactSet.

Persistence of Results

The portfolios tested consist of 10-stock baskets, sharing a common feature (such as lowest price-to-book value in our universe). Stocks are equally weighted and dividends are not included, to allow an accurate comparison with the stock index, which itself does not include dividends. For the 10-equity portfolios, we calculate both average and median performances. Moreover, to assure that the results are not dictated entirely by one or two super-stocks, the tables present what we call 8- and 9-stock averages, which are derived from the 10-equity portfolios by eliminating the single best performer in the basket or both the first and second best-performing items. We refer to these portfolios as 8-Average and 9-Average.

The 10 years from 1998 to 2008 were a roller-coaster ride for equity markets and, on the whole, terribly disappointing. Percentagewise, it was a disaster. The DJ EURO STOXX Index fell about 25 percent over the decade (dividends excluded), for an annual compound return of −2.9 percent. The late 1990s coincided with the buying climax of technology, telecom, and media stocks, followed by an equally sensational crash in 2000–2002. A new bull market blossomed in 2003, with resources, industrial, and energy sectors leading the way up. Then came the panic of 2008, which cut most exchange lists in half. Question: Were good strategies able to beat the index during both the ups and downs of the market? To find the answer, we looked at how our portfolios did in the eight periods indicated in Table 6.1. If we state that a strategy beats the market seven times out of eight, it means that in seven of those eight periods the returns of the strategy were greater than the returns of the DJ EURO STOXX Index. Table 6.1, "Single-Factor Strategies: Persistence of Results," summarizes the results.

Portfolios in Action

In the following pages we submit eight single-factor strategies to the test of time and see what happens. The single factors are price-to-earnings ratio, price-to-cashflow ratio, price-to-book ratio, dividend yield, return on equity, enterprise-value-to-sales ratio, enterprise-value-to-EBITDA ratio, and relative strength. We also tested a few multifactor approaches.

Certainly, there are other ratios, multifactor combinations, or a more detailed analysis of risk that we could have considered. But this would have given the chapter a much wider scope than was originally intended and would lead to an entire 400-page volume on backtesting, and that was not the aim of this book. We believe that our methodology and results provide a potent basis for understanding what works and does not work in Eurozone stock markets, and may open a wider discussion on the topic.

Some of the results are really very good; they may have been influenced by chance to some extent. Yet, we cannot overstate the importance of the fact that the direction of the findings is in line with what other researchers found when analyzing longer-duration databases in the United States. This reinforces our confidence in the direction of the results for Europe.

Price-to-Earnings Ratios: Not as Good as You Might Think

Buying low price-to-earnings (P/E) stocks is usually regarded as a cornerstone of value investing. Yet our evidence is mixed on its effectiveness as an investment strategy.

The P/E ratio is the number derived by taking the current price of the stock and dividing it by the company's earnings. If the stock

Table 6.1   Single-Factor Strategies: Persistence of Results (How Many Times the Strategies Beat the Market)

Period 1 From 31-Dec-1998 to 31-Dec-2001
Period 2 From 31-Dec-1999 to 31-Dec-2002
Period 3 From 31-Dec-2000 to 31-Dec-2003
Period 4 From 31-Dec-2001 to 31-Dec-2004
Period 5 From 31-Dec-2002 to 31-Dec-2005
Period 6 From 31-Dec-2003 to 31-Dec-2006
Period 7 From 31-Dec-2004 to 31-Dec-2007
Period 8 From 31-Dec-2005 to 31-Dec-2008

Summary: Single-Factor Strategies, Persistency of Results

	Price/ Earnings	Price/ Cashflow	Price/ Book	Dividend Yield
Historical Data				
10-Stock Portfolio	6/8	8/8	8/8	7/8
10-Median	6/8	7/8	8/8	5/8
9-Average	5/8	6/8	6/8	5/8
8-Average	5/8	4/8	5/8	4/8
Forecast Data				
10-Stock Portfolio	8/8	8/8	8/8	6/8
10-Median	8/8	7/8	6/8	6/8
9-Average	7/8	6/8	6/8	5/8
8-Average	4/8	4/8	5/8	5/8

	ROE	EV/ Sales	EV/ EBITDA	Relative Strength
Historical Data				
10-Stock Portfolio	3/8	8/8	8/8	6/8
10-Median	2/8	7/8	5/8	4/8
9-Average	1/8	6/8	6/8	3/8
8-Average	0/8	6/8	5/8	3/8
Forecast Data				
10-Stock Portfolio	2/8	7/8	8/8	NA
10-Median	1/8	6/8	7/8	NA
9-Average	1/8	7/8	6/8	NA
8-Average	0/8	5/8	5/8	NA

price is €100 and its earnings are €10 a share, the P/E is 10, that is, €100 divided by €10. Value investors always seek companies whose market prices are significantly below their "true" or "intrinsic" merit, believing that sooner or later investors will recognize the bargains and bid up the market prices. Hence, value investors are generally not apt to pay lofty prices in the stock market when looking at low-P/E companies is one of their favored tools.

However, a low P/E ratio is not the best gauge of value that we have tested, this outcome is consistent with longer-term analyses in the United States.

We start with a €100,000 investment in the 10 stocks with the lowest P/E ratio on December 31, 1998, and rebalance the basket every three years through December 31, 2007, so as to avoid, for now, the Great Crash of 2008. The portfolio turned €100,000 into €164,000, with an annual compound return of 5.7 percent against 3.7 percent for the DJ EURO STOXX Index. The strategy beat the market five times out of seven, and six times out of eight if 2008 is included (see Table 6.1, "Single-Factor Strategies: Persistence of Results"). But if we delete from the 10 low-P/E portfolios the best-performing stock or the two best-performing stocks, the annual compound returns worsen to 2.8 percent and −0.6 percent, respectively.

As explained in the previous pages, this chapter tests the strategies using both historical and forecast data. In the case of our low-P/E portfolio, returns increase dramatically when forecast data are employed instead of historical figures. In fact, the annual compound return rises from 5.7 to 12.2 percent. Remember that on December 31, 2001, historical earnings generally come from the 2000 balance sheet, while forecast earnings are related to the 2001 balance sheet and represent a forecast since the document will be presented only in March 2002. Thus, it might be that a low-P/E portfolio based on forecast data is more fruitful because historical data have less relevance to current market conditions; however, we have not noticed this pronounced difference for the other strategies we tested.

Finally, when we include the crash of 2008, the annual compound return of the strategy declines to −0.4 percent, if using historical data, and to 5.1 percent with forecast data. Over the same decade, the DJ EURO STOXX Index showed a compound annual return of −2.9 percent.

Price-to-Cashflow Ratios: Value with Transparency

Some value investors think that cashflows give a more accurate reflection of the current state of affairs than earnings records, because cashflows do not involve lots of assumptions (and occasional accounting hocus pocus). Cashflow equals cash receipts minus cash payments over a given period of time. Stocks with low price-to-cashflow (P/C) were a good purchase in our testing period. One hundred thousand euros invested on December 31, 1998, in the 10 stocks with the lowest P/C was worth €276,482 on December 31, 2007, for an annual compound return of 12.0 percent, far better than the DJ EURO STOXX Index return of 3.7 percent. Over the full decade, from 1998 to 2008, the annual return slid to 3.0 percent versus −2.9 percent for the stock market. The low-P/C portfolio also enjoyed great persistence of results, beating the index eight times out of eight (see Table 6.1).

Price-to-Book Ratios: Buying at Liquidation Value

The price-to-book ratio (P/B) is obtained by dividing the current price of the stock by its book value per share. Low-P/B hunters love to buy companies whose market price is close or below their liquidation value. Or, when it comes to a choice between two comparable businesses, they tend to prefer the one with a lower P/B. Critics reply that especially when there is a lot of debt on the right side of the balance sheet, overvalued assets on the left side can be treacherous, so if you buy a stock for its book value, you'd better have a detailed, first-hand understanding of what those values are all about.

In our universe of stocks, buying a basket of low-P/B equities was a rewarding strategy until 2007. We invested €100,000 on December 31, 1998, in the 10 stocks with the lowest P/B ratio and rebalanced the basket every three years until December 31, 2007, when the portfolio was worth €289,629, for an annual compound return of 12.5 percent. Until then the strategy was very stable, beating the DJ EURO STOXX Index seven times out of seven. Results were almost identical using both historical and forecast inputs and did not suffer a dramatic decay when the best performing stock or the two best-performing stocks were eliminated from the portfolio (9-Average and 8-Average, in the tables). However, the portfolio collapsed in 2008, moving back from €289,629 to €118,277, which translated into an annual return of 1.7 percent over the decade.

Dividend Yields: Betting on an Income Flow

John D. Rockefeller famously said, "Do you know the only thing that gives me pleasure? It's to see my dividends coming in." It may sound like an old-fashioned idea, but high and steady dividends are often associated with outperforming stocks in the long run. Our research leans toward the same conclusion.

You get a stock's dividend yield by dividing the annual dividend per share by the current price of the stock. If the annual dividend is €5 and the current stock price is €100, the dividend yield is 5 percent.

As usual, we put together a basket with the 10 stocks carrying the highest dividend yield and refresh the portfolio every three years. The backtesting starts on December 31, 1998, and runs its course until December 31, 2007. A hypothetical €100,000 initial stake grows to €199,974, beating the market most of the time. In 2008, the portfolio plunges to €106,827, and the annual return goes down to 0.7 percent over the decade. From a superficial inspection, that could look like a mediocre growth pace. But remember: To allow a homogeneous comparison with the DJ EURO STOXX Index, the performances of the portfolios did not include dividends, which in the present case largely distorts and underestimates the results. By how much? Over the decade, the annual dividend yield of this basket fluctuated between 5 and 8.8 percent, so the strategy was well ahead of the market when dividends are included.

Return on Equity: Poor If Taken Alone

Return-on-equity (ROE) is considered a straightforward measure of management effectiveness. You find it by dividing net income by shareholder equity. ROE sleuths look at how well a business uses investment funds to generate earnings growth: All else being equal, the higher the ROE, the better the management's ability to invest shareholders' money. Superstar investors such as Warren Buffett or John Neff have always emphasized the role of ROE in their decision making. Yet, taken alone, return on equity fails to be the hallmark of outperforming stocks. This was proven on U.S. stocks and is confirmed in our universe of Eurozone equities.

On December 31, 1998, we wrap up a portfolio of 10 stocks with the highest ROE and see how it fares until December 31, 2007. We reshuffle the basket as for the other portfolios. The results are disappointing. The compound return of the 10 high-ROE stocks was

3.6 percent when using historical data and slightly negative when employing forecast data. Equally significant, the portfolio beat a simple strategy of indexing to the DJ EURO STOXX only a minority of times. In 2008, the portfolio dropped more or less along with the market.

Enterprise Value to Sales: The Best Individual Ratio We Tested

Looking for market beating stocks by the enterprise-value-to-sales ratio is the best single-factor strategy we have tested. Value hunters tend to believe that a low enterprise value-to-sales (EV/S) is symptomatic of a bargain stock; the logic is the same as with the price-to-cash or the price-to-earnings multiples, but it compares the value of the company against its annual sales. The enterprise value is defined as market capitalization plus debt, minority interest, and preferred shares, minus total cash and cash equivalents. When calculated on a per-share basis, analysts see the EV as an alternative way of pricing a stock. In fact, some think of a company's EV as its theoretical takeover price, because the acquirer has to take on the company's debt, but could benefit from the cash position. All else being equal, the higher the debt, the higher the EV/S ratio; on the other hand, the stronger the cash position, the lower the ratio.

Betting on a portfolio consisting of the 10 stocks with the lowest EV/S ratio was a very rewarding endeavor in our testing period. From December 31, 1998 through December 31, 2007, our initial stake of €100,000 (rebalanced as usual) grew to €386,470, for a compound annual return of 16.2 percent, far better than the 3.7 percent of the index. In 2008 the portfolio came back to €217,774, for an annual compound return of 8.1 percent for the decade. The strategy was stable, beating the market eight times out of eight, and showed excellent performance both in connection with historical data and forecast inputs.

Enterprise Value to EBITDA

Another way of measuring the value of a company against its profitability is EV-to-EBITDA (EV/EBITDA). EBITDA is the acronym for "earnings before interest, taxes, depreciation, and amortization." Some analysts prefer this gauge of income when assessing the ability of a company to service its debt, or in industries where there are large amounts of assets to be written down.

In our research, low-EV/EBITDA stocks proved to be a sound investment. The portfolio including the 10 stocks with the lowest ratio delivered an annual compound return of 13.7 percent from December 31, 1998, through December 31, 2007. In that period of time, the strategy outperformed the DJ EURO STOXX Index seven times out of seven. When it came to 2008, the low-EV/EBITDA basket was almost halved, and the annual compound return landed at 5.7 percent for the decade.

Relative Strength: Run with the Bulls

As the old saying goes, nothing succeeds like success. It seems to be true in the stock market as well, where staying with the price winners from the previous year generated good profits in our testing period. Again, this outcome is not incongruous with what empirical research has observed in the United States, although it's anathema to efficient-market theorists, for whom price momentum is, of course, totally irrelevant.

We sorted stocks on relative price strength, dividing this-year-end price by last-year-end price: the higher the figure, the greater the price appreciation in the past 12 months. Then we chose the 10 stocks with the highest relative strength and formed a portfolio, to be rebalanced every three years as with the other approaches. The annual compound return of this portfolio was 14.4 percent from December 31, 1998, through December 31, 2007, and fell to 6.8 percent when the disastrous 2008 was included.

The Data

Tables 6.2 through 6.5 summarize the data that informed the strategies we presented in the previous pages, while Figure 6.1 (on page 104) illustrates the composite of these four tables.

Strategies on Steroids: When Individual Factors Cooperate

After reporting on single-factor strategies in the preceding paragraphs, we now explore combinations of two or more basic ratios. There are several ways to do so. We looked at what you might call "value with some spice." The idea was to buy stocks experiencing good market momentum (spice), but refuse to pay lofty prices

Table 6.2   Summary: Performance Before the Crash of 2008: How 100,000 Euros Invested on December 31, 1998, Fared through December 31, 2007

	Price/Earnings		Price/Cashflow	
	Total (Euros)	Annual R. (%)	Total (Euros)	Annual R. (%)
Historical Data				
10-Stock Portfolio	164,383	5.7	276,482	12.0
10-Median	140,655	3.9	196,962	7.8
9-Average	127,811	2.8	180,487	6.8
8-Average	95,031	−0.5	128,976	2.9
Forecast Data				
10-Stock Portfolio	280,920	12.6	273,573	11.8
10-Median	247,859	10.6	197,921	7.9
9-Average	215,252	8.9	170,085	6.1
8-Average	170,108	6.1	121,667	2.2
	Price/Book		Dividend Yield	
	Total (Euros)	Annual R. (%)	Total (Euros)	Annual R. (%)
Historical Data				
10-Stock Portfolio	289,629	12.5	199,974	8.0
10-Median	234,329	9.9	143,422	4.1
9-Average	185,510	7.1	144,888	4.2
8-Average	140,720	3.9	121,538	2.2
Forecast Data				
10-Stock Portfolio	311,142	13.4	221,576	9.2
10-Median	226,312	9.5	199,062	8.0
9-Average	187,239	7.2	164,573	5.7
8-Average	137,285	3.6	139,718	3.8
Benchmark				
DJ EURO STOXX Index	139,056	3.7		

The table summarizes the results of the first four strategies based on a single factor. The period is from 1998 through 2007, namely before the crash of 2008. For each strategy, the table illustrates the final value of €100,000 invested in the 10-stock portfolio and its annual return. "10-Median" is for the median return of the same basket, while "9-Average" and "8-Average" are obtained by deleting from the 10-stock portfolio the best-performing and the two best-performing stocks, respectively. Strategies are calculated both on historical and forecast data.

Table 6.3   Summary: Performance Before the Crash of 2008: How 100,000 Euros Invested on December 31, 1998, Fared through December 31, 2007

	ROE		EV/Sales	
	Total (Euros)	Annual R. (%)	Total (Euros)	Annual R. (%)
Historical Data				
10-Stock Portfolio	137,696	3.6	386,470	16.2
10-Median	137,505	3.6	286,318	11.6
9-Average	99,199	–0.1	261,057	11.3
8-Average	78,308	–2.7	193,799	7.6
Forecast Data				
10-Stock Portfolio	92,567	–0.9	342,690	14.7
10-Median	98,728	–0.1	196,453	7.8
9-Average	68,457	–4.1	238,198	10.1
8-Average	57,346	–6.0	174,008	6.4

	EV/EBITDA		Relative Strength	
	Total (Euros)	Annual R. (%)	Total (Euros)	Annual R. (%)
Historical Data				
10-Stock Portfolio	316,361	13.7	335,642	14.4
10-Median	208,196	8.5	249,881	10.7
9-Average	207,577	8.5	212,706	8.8
8-Average	145,248	4.2	157,530	5.2
Forecast Data				
10-Stock Portfolio	274,658	11.9	NA	NA
10-Median	205,627	8.3	NA	NA
9-Average	180,122	6.8	NA	NA
8-Average	123,651	2.4	NA	NA
Benchmark				
DJ EURO STOXX Index	139,056	3.7		

The table summarizes the results of the second four strategies based on a single factor. The period is from 1998 through 2007, namely before the crash of 2008. For each strategy, the table illustrates the final value of €100,000 invested in the 10-stock portfolio and its annual return. "10-Median" is for the median return of the same basket, while "9-Average" and "8-Average" are obtained by deleting from the 10-stock portfolio the best-performing and the two best-performing stocks, respectively. Strategies are calculated both on historical and forecast data.

Table 6.4   Summary: Performance Including the Crash of 2008: How 100,000 Euros Invested on December 31, 1998, Fared through December 31, 2008

	Price/Earnings		Price/Cashflow	
	Total (Euros)	Annual R. (%)	Total (Euros)	Annual R. (%)
Historical Data				
10-Stock Portfolio	96,414	−0.4	134,861	3.0
10-Median	72,673	−3.1	93,367	−0.7
9-Average	60,550	−4.9	83,466	−1.8
8-Average	43,291	−8.0	56,964	−5.5
Forecast Data				
10-Stock Portfolio	163,956	5.1	112,873	1.2
10-Median	128,005	2.5	79,995	−2.2
9-Average	101,284	0.1	66,091	−4.1
8-Average	76,878	−2.6	43,846	−7.9

	Price/Book		Dividend Yield	
	Total (Euros)	Annual R. (%)	Total (Euros)	Annual R. (%)
Historical Data				
10-Stock Portfolio	118,277	1.7	106,827	0.7
10-Median	74,542	−2.9	75,579	−2.8
9-Average	64,900	−4.2	71,578	−3.3
8-Average	40,553	−8.6	56,423	−5.6
Forecast Data				
10-Stock Portfolio	115,536	1.5	113,470	1.3
10-Median	78,189	−2.4	103,011	0.3
9-Average	62,544	−4.6	77,262	−2.6
8-Average	40,486	−8.7	61,003	−4.8
Benchmark				
DJ EURO STOXX Index	74,676	−2.9		

The table summarizes the results of the first four strategies based on a single factor. The period is from 1998 through 2008, that is, including the crash of 2008. For each strategy, the table illustrates the final value of €100,000 invested in the 10-stock portfolio and its annual return. "10-Median" is for the median return of the same basket, while "9-Average" and "8-Average" are obtained by deleting from the 10-stock portfolio the best-performing and the two best-performing stocks, respectively. Strategies are calculated both on historical and forecast data.

Table 6.5 Summary: Performance Including the Crash of 2008: How 100,000 Euros Invested on December 31, 1998, Fared through December 31, 2008

	ROE		EV/Sales	
	Total (Euros)	Annual R. (%)	Total (Euros)	Annual R. (%)
Historical Data				
10-Stock Portfolio	78,928	−2.3	217,774	8.1
10-Median	69,144	−3.6	110,285	1.0
9-Average	50,026	−6.3	116,994	1.6
8-Average	38,821	−9.3	80,580	−2.1
Forecast Data				
10-Stock Portfolio	59,072	−5.1	161,009	4.9
10-Median	65,543	−4.1	96,792	−0.3
9-Average	40,844	−8.6	105,635	0.6
8-Average	32,510	−10.6	72,459	−3.2

	EV/EBITDA		Relative Strength	
	Total (Euros)	Annual R. (%)	Total (Euros)	Annual R. (%)
Historical Data				
10-Stock Portfolio	173,961	5.7	192,917	6.8
10-Median	83,603	−1.8	98,043	−0.2
9-Average	89,887	−1.1	97,991	−0.2
8-Average	58,776	−5.2	62,299	−4.6
Forecast Data				
10-Stock Portfolio	123,248	2.1		
10-Median	92,110	−0.8	NA	NA
9-Average	76,599	−2.6	NA	NA
8-Average	49,664	−6.8	NA	NA
Benchmark				
DJ EURO STOXX Index	74,676	−2.9		

The table summarizes the results of the second four strategies based on a single factor. The period is from 1998 through 2008, that is, including the crash of 2008. For each strategy, the table illustrates the final value of €100,000 invested in the 10-stock portfolio and its annual return. "10-Median" is for the median return of the same basket, while "9-Average" and "8-Average" are obtained by deleting from the 10-stock portfolio the best-performing and the two best-performing stocks, respectively. Strategies are calculated both on historical and forecast data.

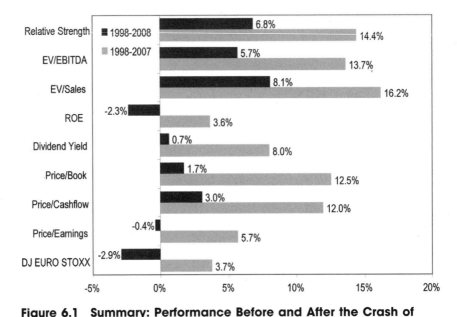

Figure 6.1   Summary: Performance Before and After the Crash of 2008—How 100,000 Euros Invested on December 31, 1998 Fared through December 31, 2007, and through December 31, 2008

Note: The figure shows the performance of the 10-stock portfolios to the DJ EURO STOXX Index during both periods, from 1998 through 2007 and from 1998 through 2008, that is to say, exclusive and inclusive of the crash of 2008.

(value). Once again, the general approach is not new and was successfully tested in the United States on longer databases. With similar tools you may find startling nuggets in the Eurozone as well.

Here are three multifactor portfolios we tested and their performances:

Strategy 1: Buy the 10 stocks with the best price appreciation from the previous year, but never pay more than 15 times (historical) earnings. This is a simple and classical way to combine one growth ratio and one value ratio. The low-P/E multiple serves as a sieve to filter out potentially overvalued companies. Of course, the filter is not bombproof and, especially in 2008, many overvalued stocks had low P/Es because the "E" part was inflated: Homebuilders offered a perfect illustration. The latter rule of the strategy consists of buying the 10 stocks that appreciated the most in the previous year, in accordance with the old saying that "the trend is your friend."

As for the single-factor portfolios, we began the study on December 31, 1998, with a €100,000 stake in the 10 equities fulfilling the rules, and rebalancing the portfolio every three years through December 31, 2007. At this point the portfolio was worth €285,766, for a compound growth rate of 12.4 percent per year. In the same period, the DJ EURO STOXX Index delivered a compound annual return of 3.7 percent, turning the initial €100,000 into €139,057. Then came the slaughter of 2008, when both the strategy and the benchmark took a bloodbath: The strategy plummeted by some 57 percent, against 46 percent for the DJ EURO STOXX. It is worth observing that none of the approaches in this chapter managed to prevent the hypothetical investor from losing tons of money in 2008. Some did better and some did worse, but we see little more than chance here. This reminds us how ferocious, pitiless, and (hopefully) unusual the 2008 bear market was.

However, to get back to the point, the marriage of low P/E ratios and strong price momentum resulted in a market-beating profit over the whole decade from December 31, 1998, to December 31, 2008, with an annual compound return of 2.1 percent against −2.9 percent for the overall market.

Strategy 2:   The rules of our second multifactor strategy are as follows: Buy the 10 stocks with the highest price appreciation from the previous year but be sure that their price-to-cash-flow ratio is below 10 and the dividend yield is greater than 2 percent. The combination of low price-to-cashflow ratio and high dividend yield gravitates us toward companies paying good money to the shareholder and whose cashflow is not paid excessively. The results are encouraging in our testing period. An initial portfolio of €100,000 created on December 31, 1998, and refreshed every three years, jumped to €491,916 on December 31, 2007, for an annual compound return of 19.4 percent. In 2008, the portfolio came back to €285,000, which translated to a fantastic 11.1 percent against an annual loss of 2.9 percent for the index. Such a huge positive gap likely carries with it a good dose of luck, but the results were still positive even when we slightly changed the mechanics of the experiment. For instance, rebalancing the portfolio every two years instead of our customary three years, the annual compound return slid to 8.7 percent, which is still a considerable achievement.

Strategy 3: For the third strategy, cheap companies are sorted out from the entire universe of stocks by a combination of factors. Price/earnings, price/book, and price/cashflow had to be below the median value of the universe, while dividend yield had to be above the median threshold. (This might sound confusing, but the rules are actually simple, because all of them point in the same direction: value). From the resulting basket, the portfolio was constructed by electing the 10 stocks with the highest price appreciation from the previous 12 months. Again, it is value with some spice.

Table 6.6 Summary of Results for Multifactor Strategies: How 100,000 Euros Invested on December 31, 1998, Fared through December 31, 2007, and through December 31, 2008

	From 1998 (Euros)	To 2007 (Euros)	Annual R. (%)	To 2008 (Euros)	Annual R. (%)
Strategy 1 Best price winners 0 < P/E < 15	100,000	285,766	12.4	122,927	2.1
Strategy 2 Best price winners P/CF < 10, DY > 2%	100,000	491,920	19.4	285,919	11.1
Strategy 3 Best price winners P/E, P/B, P/CF < median, DY > Median	100,000	410,000	17.0	222,999	8.4
DJ EURO STOXX	100,000	139,000	3.7	74,673	−2.9

Let's see what happens when the strategy is submitted to the test of time. From December 31, 1998, through December 31, 2007, €100,000 invested in the 10-stock portfolio moved up to €410,000, for an annual growth rate of 17.0 percent. Including 2008, the annual return slowed down to 8.4 percent, against a loss of 2.9 percent for the stock index (see Table 6.6).

CHAPTER 7

Valuation

Mirror, mirror on the wall, who in the land is fairest of all?

—Snow White

If you believe that "buying cheap" offers tremendous opportunities in the long run, Europe is a place you simply cannot afford to disregard. By many measures, the Old Continent looks cheap in absolute terms; and, by many measures, it looks equally cheap, or even super-cheap, compared to Wall Street. When Europe is selling at a deep discount from the United States, the odds are historically high that, sooner or later, it will outperform its American counterpart, diminishing the valuation gap. This is true in normal times. It ought to be even more true if our contention is valid that American stocks deserve a smaller premium since the country has embarked on more social-democratic, less free-market-oriented policies.

Europe at an All-Time Low

What does it mean that Europe is cheap against the United States? It means that, in the summer of 2009, relative market multiples were hovering at the bottom end of their multi-decade trading range. For instance, European price-to-earnings ratios (P/E) were some 60 to 65 percent of the U.S. ratio. This was close to the lowest level in

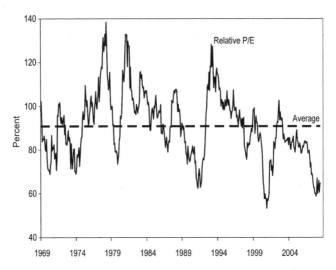

Figure 7.1 MSCI Europe Close to Trough Relative P/E against MSCI USA, December 1969–July 2009

Source: MSCI, Morgan Stanley Research; reprinted with permission.

almost 40 years (see Figure 7.1). We are referring to an ample representation of European securities here, measured by the MSCI Europe Index, which covers the United Kingdom as well. Over the decades, the relative P/E, using 12-month trailing data, has been oscillating between 60 and 130 percent, with an average value of about 90 percent, that is, at a small premium in favor of the United States.

Europe has also been trading at a low point when you consider the nominal Shiller P/E ratio, the multiple you get by dividing the current market price by a long-term average of earnings. By using a long-term average, an investor is able to smooth the cycle and form an idea of what companies earn through the hills and valleys of the business cycle. Against the Shiller P/E ratio, Europe has been near an all-time low relative to Wall Street (see Figure 7.2).

On top of that, European dividends have been very substantial, which is important after Enron and all the shenanigans the world has witnessed in recent years. In light of those painful experiences, perhaps investors will look for somewhat higher dividends than usual as a tangible sign that earnings do not live only in the gymnastics of the accounting wizards. From this point of view, Europe's dividends have been some 80 percent higher than on the American side of the Atlantic and higher than in Japan and in the emerging

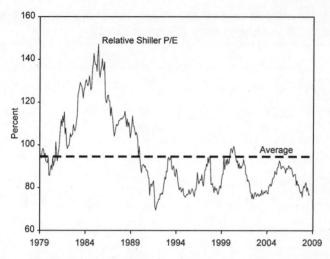

Figure 7.2   MSCI Europe Relative to MSCI USA: Shiller P/E Close to Lows, November 1979–July 2009
Note: Price to 10-year average EPS.
Source: MSCI, Morgan Stanley Research; reprinted with permission.

markets as a whole (always using the MSCI indexes). Further, most of the international stock markets yielding high dividends were located in the Old Continent (see Table 7.1).

According to research from Morgan Stanley, in the summer of 2009, the valuation gap between Europe and the United States was close to a 35-year low.[1] The brokerage house showed that, by an average of three multiples, Europe was 35 percent cheaper than the United States, which had happened only 8 percent of the time in almost 40 years of data. Morgan Stanley took an average of the price-to-book ratio, the price-to-cash-earnings ratio, and the price-to-dividend-yield ratio on 12-month trailing data and referred to the MSCI Europe universe versus the MSCI USA counterpart (see Table 7.2). The study also noted that, on a sector-neutral valuation, the Old Continent was at a five- to seven-year low, namely cheaper than the United States, but not so extremely as in the first case.

Moving our attention to the Eurozone, the tables and the charts in the following pages depict a stock market that is attractive by most traditional multiples. The price-to-book ratio for the DJ EURO STOXX was at an all-time low in the history of the common currency and very depressed against the United States (see Figures 7.3 and 7.4). The dividend yield, staying at 4 percent, exceeded 10-year

Table 7.1   Dividends around the World: European Markets Pay Well—Major Markets with High Dividend Yields

Benchmark	Country	Dividend Yield (%)
IPSA (CL)	Chile	5.6
NZSX 15 (NZ)	New Zealand	5.5
Ibex 35 (ES)	Spain	5.1
PX 50 (CZ)	Czech Republic	5.1
S&P/ASX 100 Index Full Share (AU)	Australia	4.5
DJ EURO STOXX 50	Euroland	4.4
DJ Stoxx 50	EU + CH + NO	4.3
FTSE 100 (GB)	Great Britain	4.2
CAC 40 (FR)	France	4.2
PSI 20 (PT)	Portugal	4.2
DJ Euro Stoxx	Euroland	4.0
OMXH25 (FI)	Finland	4.0
FTSE/MIB (IT)	Italy	3.9
FTSE Athex 20 (GR)	Greece	3.8
SET 50 (TH)	Thailand	3.8
DAX Price (DE)	Germany	3.7
PSE (PH)	Philippines	3.6
Luxx (LU) (Inactive)	Luxembourg	3.3
FTSE/JSE Top 40 (ZA)	South Africa	3.2
FTSE Straits Times (SG)	Singapore	3.2

Source: FactSet, July 2009.

Table 7.2   MSCI Europe versus MSCI USA Valuation: Relative Multiples in Bottom Decile of History in Many Classes

	Price to Earnings	Price to Cash Earnings	Price to Book	Price to Dividend	Average of P/E, P/CE, P/Div
MSCI Europe	11.1	5.9	1.4	22.9	
MSCI USA	18.6	8.2	2.0	41.8	
Europe Relative to USA	0.6	0.7	0.7	0.6	0.7
Historical Average Relative Valuation	0.9	0.7	0.8	0.8	0.8
Percentile of Relative Valuation	2	40	22	2	8

Source: Morgan Stanley; reprinted with permission, June 2009.

Figure 7.3   DJ EURO STOXX Price to Book: January 1996–July 2009
Source: FactSet.

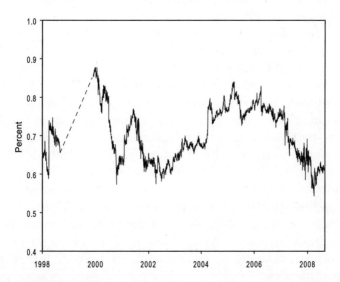

**Figure 7.4   Relative Price to Book: DJ EURO STOXX to S&P 500,
January 1998–July 2009**
Source: FactSet.

Table 7.3   Europe's Market Multiples Are Cheap

Benchmarks	Net Dividend Yield		Price/Earnings		Price/Book		Ret On Equity	
	2009 Div Yld	10-yr Average	2009 P/E	10-yr Average	2009 P/B	10-yr Average	2009 ROE	10-yr Average
DJ EURO STOXX, Euroland	4.0%	3.0%	14.2x	16.1x	1.3x	2.1x	9.0%	13.5%
S&P 500, U.S.	2.3	1.8	16.2	18.3	2.1	2.8	12.6	16.0
Nikkei 225, Japan	1.7	1.1	60.6	25.4	1.3	1.7	2.2	7.4
FTSE All-Emerging, World	2.4	2.9	15.3	11.4	1.8	1.7	11.8	15.1

Source: FactSet, estimates 2009 in July 2009.

German bund yields by 60 basis points. The volatile price-to-earnings ratio enjoyed a 12 percent discount from its 10-year average. And, vis-à-vis the United States, the aforementioned multiples went through a greater improvement against their respective 10-year averages. (See Figure 7.4 and Table 7.3, calculated in July 2009 on 2009 FactSet consensus data.)

When should Europe and Eurozone markets start to outperform because of the valuation gap? The general rule is that the Old Continent tends to proceed somewhat like a cyclical stock, accelerating as soon as the economy recovers its poise and then keeping an elevated rhythm when activity warms up and, finally, overheats. Perfect illustrations are the recovery phase of 1992–1993 or the raging bull markets of 1999–2000 and 2003–2007. If the pattern holds, Europe ought to catch up in the course of the next economic revival and/or global bull market (which may be in its early stages as this book is published). But if the pattern is broken or if the economy falls back once again, European stocks ought to demonstrate some resistance, at least compared to Wall Street, due to depressed metrics.

It was the bear market that culminated in March 2009 that led Europe's valuations to their extreme low against the United States. In fact, it sparked the mother of all stampedes out of the Old Continent. Remember, in 2007 global investors were largely overweighting

Eurozone equities.[2] Then came the crash of 2008, and asset allocators repatriated money. Large American banks needed money in their coffers and disgorged their positions abroad. Selling stocks and parking liquidity in government obligations—preferably U.S. short-term securities—was the vogue in 2008. The process went on and on until, in March 2009, a net 40 percent of respondents to a Bank of America-Merrill Lynch survey stated that they were underweighting Eurozone equities.[3] Just a few quarters earlier, they were copiously overweighting. The pendulum had moved from one extreme to the other. The entire investment world had dumped Europe.

And, of course, Eurozone households manifested an equally deep-rooted dislike for domestic stocks. In March 2009, cash positions, defined as money market funds plus notice deposits, went well beyond the record reached during the selling climax of 2002. As a percentage of euro area equity-market capitalization, cash exceeded 80 percent. In some Eurozone countries, savings allocated to equity mutual funds were of the same magnitude as the ones left in money market funds. By contrast, when stocks were hot, for instance in the year 2000, the ratio was sometimes five or seven euros to equity market funds, 1 euro to money market funds.[4] Early in 2009, the scramble to sell stocks battered prices to depression levels. Take the case of Italy as a vivid example. At the bottom of March 2009, its equity market, when adjusted for inflation, plunged some 20 to 30 percent below the peaks of 1961 and 1943. And that includes dividends. Think of it: In 1943 Italy was still under the leadership of Benito Mussolini, and in 1961 the country was celebrating its first after-war industrial bloom. Yet in March 2009 stocks sank well below those levels (see Figure 7.5).

Earnings Cycle

Over the last 50 years there have been five major earnings cycles in Europe (the UK included): one in the mid-1970s, one in the early 1980s, one in the early 1990s, one in the early 2000s, and—last but not least—one in the late 2000s, culminating (hopefully) somewhere between 2009 and early 2010. In 2008 earnings fell by 24.2 percent, and FactSet consensus data expects another 18.1 percent drop in 2009 (see Figure 7.6). For the Eurozone, the figures were −27.1 percent and −19.9 percent, respectively. If reality does not exceed consensus expectations too much, the cumulative decline will show

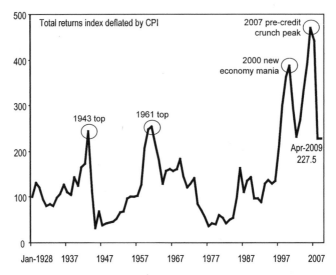

Figure 7.5   Italy's Stock Market Plunged below Mussolini's Peak, January 1928–April 2009
Source: Mediobanca Research Department; reprinted with permission.

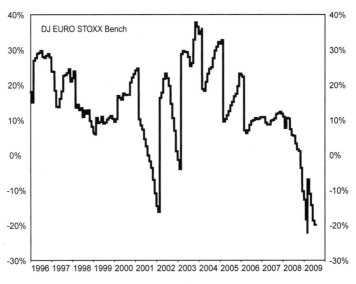

Figure 7.6   DJ EURO STOXX: Change in earnings per share, January 1996–July 2009
Source: FactSet.

a close similarity with past experiences, since in the mid-1970s, in the early 1990s, and in the early 2000s, earnings slid by some 40 percent, while in the early 1980s the fall stopped at around 30 percent.

According to calculations by Citigroup, on average it took about 30 months for earnings to regain pre-downturn peaks, starting from the bottom level.[5] Moreover, Citigroup's analysts showed that after the trough, earnings usually advanced at a rapid rate. They considerd the four cycles aforementioned and added the cycle of the early 1970s. On average, the earnings growth rate surpassed 20 percent per annum in each of the four years following the trough. The entire upleg of the cycle lasted 5 to 10 years, with earnings rising 200 percent.[6]

Since multiples were undemanding in the summer of 2009, earnings growth ought to be another driver of market appreciation in the next few years—unless this time is really different and the downleg of the earnings cycle largely transgresses the constraints of past experiences, annihilating profits.

If Americans Sell Wall Street and Buy Abroad

There is a clamorous hue and cry among foreign governments about the role of the dollar as a reserve currency. Central bankers ranging from China to Brazil and from Russia to India have warned that if the United States insists on a "printing and spending" policy, the great international role of the dollar may be questioned. And there is no doubt that the malaise is serious and genuine. A number of observers have begun giving less and less credibility to the willingness of U.S. authorities to keep inflation at bay, to preserve the purchasing power of the dollar.

But there's another truth that is not as widely recognized: American holders of financial assets are the first to be preoccupied with the trajectory of their currency. Even the savvy Warren Buffett took a large position against the buck in 2002, apparently fearing that an expanding trade deficit would set the stage for a lower exchange rate. Before 2008, U.S. investors had been steadily diversifying out of domestic stock markets, as they fought to protect their portfolios from a persistent decline in the dollar's value. According to the Boston Fed's *Monthly Mutual Fund Report,* the ratio of "total assets world equity funds" to "total assets equity funds" rose from 14 percent in December 2003 to 23.4 percent in May 2007. In other words, Americans were diversifying out of Wall Street, and, not surprisingly, the shift went hand in hand with an outperformance of the Dow Jones Global Index to the Dow Jones Industrial Average.[7] Of course, Europe benefited from the trend: The percentage of U.S. funds investing at least 3 percent of their assets in the Eurozone rose from 13.5 percent in 2005 to 18.4 percent in 2008.[8]

According to a study by Stephen Jen,[9] as of early 2007, U.S. real-money accounts held $20.7 trillion—close to four times the size of worldwide official foreign reserves. This group of managers encompassed mutual funds, life insurers, private pension plans, and state and local pension funds. Their assets were tracked by the Fed's *Flow of Funds Report.* Mr. Jen did not have a breakdown of the asset allocation for all four categories, but noted that the Boston Fed's *Monthly Mutual Fund Report* showed a significant jump in mutual funds' allocation to international equities. He argued that by applying the same allocation to the entire group of real-money accounts, the cumulative outflows from 2003 to early 2007 could have totaled over $1 trillion, a quite impressive amount of money, although the figure was intended as a rough calculation. Equally significant, Mr. Jen noted that European investors had not embarked on a similar wholesale diversification out of Eurozone stocks.

Other sources tended to confirm that before the 2008 crash, U.S. players were moving capital abroad: According to industry analysis,[10] U.S. pension funds augmented the weight of international equities from 13.9 percent in 2005 to 17.9 percent in 2007, while the weighting of U.S. equities declined from 46.7 percent to 41.7 percent. As an example, New Jersey's pension fund had 50 percent of its portfolio in U.S. equities as of the summer of 2005, cut back to 35.6 percent in December 2007, and had a medium-term goal of 25 percent. At the same time, the share of international equities rose from 16.2 percent in June 2005 to 18.9 percent in December 2007, with a medium-term goal of 19.7 percent (see Table 7.4). The dollar was clearly on its way down, and the S&P 500 lagged behind several international bourses during 2003–2007. The performance of Eurozone averages was especially noticeable over this period of time. From January 2003 to December 2007, the DJ EURO STOXX gained 122 percent, versus 77 percent for the S&P 500 (dividends included). And that was in local currency. If measured in euros, the S&P 500 advanced by a meager 26 percent, paling against its European cousin (+122%).

Table 7.4 New Jersey Pension Fund

Asset Class	Jun. 2005	Dec. 2007	Medium Term Goal
U.S. Equities	50.0	35.6	25.0
International Equities	16.2	18.9	19.7
Emerging Markets Equities	0.0	0.3	2.5
U.S. Fixed Income	26.2	26.3	23.8
U.S. High Yield	0.0	0.3	4.0
International Fixed Income	2.2	1.8	0.0
Commodities/Real Assets	0.0	1.1	4.0
TIPs	0.0	2.8	3.0
Private Equity	0.0	2.8	5.0
Real Estate	0.0	1.8	4.0
Absolute Return	0.0	3.7	6.0
Cash	5.4	4.6	3.0

Note: Values as percentages of portfolio.
Source: William Clark, Director of Investment, State of New Jersey, May 13, 2008, Global Interdependence Center conference in Paris.

In 2008, the credit crunch abruptly reversed the outflow of capital. U.S. money managers repatriated their funds, and the movement was accompanied by a dollar rally. Eurozone indexes plunged more deeply than Wall Street. From January 2008 to March 2009, the S&P 500 lost 43.9 percent against 51.7 percent for the DJ EURO STOXX. But in common currency the gap was even wider, since the DJ EURO STOXX dropped by 56.2 percent in dollars. However, one could argue that the phenomenon is likely to be transitory, and diversification away from the United States could regain momentum in 2010, because the underlying motive power that encouraged U.S. financial players to buy foreign stocks is perhaps even more compelling in 2010 than in 2003–2007. Back then, investors were scared by profligate U.S. policies—both monetary and fiscal. In 2003–2007, it had become fashionable to say that President Bush spent all the money Chairman Greenspan could print. In reaction to the Nasdaq debacle and the Twin Towers terrorist attack, the Federal Reserve poured massive amounts of money into the system, driving interest rates to remarkably low levels. The fiscal budget moved sharply into expansionary mode. Investors were preoccupied, and justifiably so, with the possible impact of a falling dollar. They moved to protect their portfolios, buying commodities and diversifying into foreign stocks and currencies. This was a period when global managers were largely underweighting U.S. stocks and overweighting Eurozone markets.[11]

That tendency could resurface with renewed vigor from 2010 on, since investors are aware of the dangers inherent in U.S. policies that are by far more lenient now than during the Bush–Greenspan tenure. True, in 2008 governments adopted an unprecedented expansionary posture all over the world, because there was a possibility that the burden of deflationary forces could come crashing down, setting off a 1929-style economic depression. However, the Eurozone never reached the extremes of the United States as far as government policies were concerned. In the eye of the financial storm, the European Central Bank never undertook quantitative easing like the Federal Reserve did and kept its basic interest rate a little bit higher than its U.S. counterpart's (1 percent against almost 0 percent). Likewise, Eurozone governments relaxed their grip on fiscal policies, but not as much as Washington did. BCA Research has calculated on IMF data that the debt-to-GDP ratio in the Eurozone will increase by 22 percent versus 36 percent in the United States by 2014, with a less negative impact on long-term government interest rates.[12]

Whither America?

There is a vigorous discussion about the likely effects of these exceptionally accommodative policies over the next few years. Some claim that with so much easy money sloshing around the United States, the path of least resistance leads to higher inflation in the United States, accompanied by a weaker dollar. Others argue that when the economy recovers its poise, liquidity and public spending can be reduced without much damage to the economy and the taxpayer. However, we find it difficult to believe that if the expansionary policies of Alan Greenspan and George Bush prompted U.S. investors to look for diversification abroad, the far more expansionary policies of Ben Bernanke and Barack Obama will not stimulate a new wave of diversification away from Wall Street, particularly when the economy picks up and inflation pressures intensify. In the summer of 2009 Warren Buffett and Bill Gross, two of the most celebrated U.S. investors, warned that if government policies do not become less loose, the consequences for the dollar may be heavy and long-lasting.[13]

There's nothing new in these economic and political behaviors; they have happened throughout mankind's history. It was A.D. 301 when the Roman emperor Diocletian issued an *Edictum de pretiis,* turning decisively toward socialistic policies. The government enlarged its role in the economy to the point of dwarfing the private sector. A vast campaign of public works was commenced in order to give the unemployed jobs (sound familiar?), taxes shot up, and industries and other activities were either seized by the public hand or put under detailed control. The rest of the private economy languished under heavy taxation. Of course, Diocletian was not a lunatic, nor a madman like Nero; and when those in the business sector warned that the economy would be ruined by the new course, he answered that the barbarians were at the gate, poverty was on the rise, and the masses were agitated. In short, he had his good reasons. And there are always good reasons. But, good or bad, the result is the same. We are told[14] that affluent Romans crossed the borders looking for refuge among the barbarians, or hid their wealth in remote provinces where the tax collectors would not find it. In modern parlance, they diversified out of the Roman currency and assets.

Now, we are not anticipating a gloomy path for the U.S. economy, not at all. But whenever states—empires, if you wish—engage in very profligate policies, run large and increasing budget deficits, raise taxes, and stand head and shoulders above private industrialists in the control of entire segments of the economy, people—especially wealthy people—start to diversify. It happened to Rome, it might happen to the United States, if policies do not change. This does not translate to a bear-market prophecy for Wall Street. New York stock indexes may very well enjoy a new cyclical or long-term bull market, but in common currency they run the risk of underperforming, because of diversification and because the premium U.S. markets used to enjoy may taper off.

There is a possible parallel with the bull market of 2003–2007, when the DJ EURO STOXX Index gained 122 percent versus just 26 percent for the S&P 500 (common currency, see above). In 2002–2003, Europe was cheap against the United States due to selling pressures caused by the severe bear market of 2000–2002. On an average of price-to-book, price-to-cash-earnings, and price-to-dividend, Europe's valuation relative to its American counterpart was similar to the ratio in the summer of 2009. If holders of financial assets start to fear that U.S. government policies are more inflationary than Eurozone policies, they may have a strong inducement to overweight Eurozone markets and underweight Wall Street, as happened in 2003–2007. The combination of a cheap market and the inflow of international capital may lead to an outperformance of Eurozone markets. And—just as important—even if the course of events deviates from our conceptual framework, the damage to investors should be minimal, because Europe is bought on depressed metrics.

CHAPTER 8

Old Continent Stocks and the Super-Euro

Forecasting is difficult, especially about the future.

—Niels Bohr

As we discussed earlier, in 2003–2007 Eurozone stocks outperformed their U.S. cousins both in local and in common currencies. At the time, many professional analysts were doubtful about the emergence and survival of a powerful bull advance in Europe, because experience had taught them that a declining greenback was generally associated with a disappointing stock market in Europe, and vice versa. In fact, the statistics were stringent. A Morgan Stanley study identified 14 weak dollar phases since 1971, and in 10 of them MSCI Europe was down.[1] In general, a weak dollar put the European tradable sector under pressure and often signaled poor economic activity in the United States—the major market for Old Continent exporters. Yet, 2003–2007 disproved this old pattern and turned out to be a wonderful time to play the European stock market. A benign circle was set in motion in which a strong euro and a strong bourse ran together. Question: Can it happen all over again? Can Old Continent indexes move up if the dollar moves down? What were the fundamental dissimilarities between 2003–2007 and past dollar cycles that allowed Eurozone-listed companies to shrug off a falling greenback and quickly go through the roof?

For starters, the Eurozone represents a large and open economy. In 2008, extra euro exports of goods fluctuated around 16 percent of GDP, while the United States was less export-oriented at 9 percent.[2] Further, the Eurozone trade balance has not deteriorated much, despite the road-roller strength of the common currency. The July 2009 issue of *The Economist* noted that in the previous 12 months, the euro area trade deficit had been just $46.2 bn, against $674.4 bn for the United States. Throughout the 2000s, a radical shift in Eurozone commerce patterns has been underway.

European Strength in Emerging Markets

First, a large domestic market has gained confidence in the common currency, and intra-euro exports of goods, amounting to some 16 percent of GDP, are not directly affected by the dollar's move. Then, the tie with the Anglo-Saxon world has become less and less relevant as new sources of demand have been surfacing. A strong export performance to the so-called BRIC countries built up, until, in 2008, the combination of Brazil, Russia, India, and China exceeded the United States as a market outlet for the single-currency area (see Figure 8.1).

In 2000, the United States still absorbed some 17 to 18 percent of Eurozone goods, while the BRICs were in their childhood at 7 to 8 percent. Take May 2009 as a reference and relative strength had reversed: The BRICs absorbed 13.4 percent while the United States stayed at 12.1 percent. A press release underlined that, in the first half of 2009, Volkswagen sold more cars in China than in Germany, 652,000 vehicles against 630,190. An HSBC report pointed out that Adidas, the world's second largest sporting-goods maker, found in China its leading market for earnings and its second for revenue.[3] Of course, such trends are global, but they show how the impact of the United States on Eurozone economic activity isn't as great as it was during the 1980s or 1990s. Readers can also observe the diminishing role of the United States and UK combined. Early in the 2000s the two Anglo-Saxon countries received 35 to 40 percent of Eurozone exports. In May 2009 the share had slipped to 25.9 percent. By contrast, other regions are on the rise.

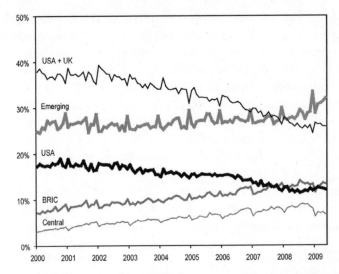

Figure 8.1   Eurozone Exports: Anglo-Saxons Down, Emerging World Up

Note: The chart depicts the trend in exports for the Eurozone toward some of the main commercial blocks. The United States and the United Kingdom are declining percentagewise, while the emerging world has been gaining share; BRIC: Brazil + Russia + India + China; Emerging: Asia – Japan + Latin America + Africa; Central: Community of Independent States + Central and Eastern Europe; USA: United States of America; USA + UK: United States of America + United Kingdom. Source: Our calculations on Eurostat data.

Figure 8.1 labels as "Emerging" the block of Asia ex Japan, Latin America, and Africa. Combined, they accounted for 25 percent of Eurozone exports at the turn of the new millennium but increased to 32 percent in May 2009, outweighing the joined markets of the United States and the United Kingdom. On top of that, there is central and eastern Europe, the immense territory spanning from the borders of the Eurozone to the former Soviet Union. The relation between core and eastern Europe went through a boom-burst sequence: Eurozone exports rose from 3 percent in 2000 to 9 percent in early 2008, but thereafter they plunged back to some 6.5 percent when eastern Europe endured the combination of a credit crunch and currency crisis (see Figure 8.1). For a detailed analysis of these interactions and specific investment theses, please read the "Guru" chapters.

In short, Europe was and is one of the main beneficiaries of the opening up of China, Eastern Europe, and the New World. About 50 percent of Eurozone exports of goods go to emerging markets, roughly the same share as for the United States. But since exports are a much greater part of Old Continent GDP, the exposure to emerging markets is proportionally larger.[4] On the other hand, core Europe suffered a severe setback in 2008 when emerging countries went into a tailspin and Eastern Europe sent a shiver through the banking channel. However, the United States is no longer the only driving force for Eurozone exports. Therefore, it is conceivable that the emergence and development of a bull market in the Old Continent can coexist with a weak dollar. It is even plausible that the U.S. share of global imports will decline further, if American households go on a saving spree, as many observers expect. According to economist Gary Shilling, a 1 percent rise in U.S. consumer spending is matched by a 2.8 percent rise in U.S. imports,[5] but the opposite is also true. Hence, if households tighten their belts in order to restore financial balance, imports are likely to taper off and Eurozone exports may be affected negatively. Regarding the implications for the dollar of a rising saving rate in the United States, please read the "Guru" chapters.

Changes in trade flows are reflected in corporate earnings and revenue. Morgan Stanley has defined "emerging markets" as the world ex the United States, Canada, developed Europe, and Japan.[6] By this definition, in 2007, European companies generated more revenue from emerging markets than from North America. Morgan Stanley's study showed a detailed analysis of the changes in 2004–2007 (see Tables 8.1 and 8.2), a period that the authors of this book think may provide a roadmap for the next few years when worldwide economic activity picks up and emerging markets are likely to become one of the main sources of growth. In 2004–2007, European companies' exposure to emerging markets (as defined by Morgan Stanley) rose from 16.1 to 21.2 percent, while the share that originated in developed Europe declined from 64.9 to 61.8 percent and that of North America from 17.6 to 15.9 percent. As one would expect, small caps were more Europe-centric, with over 70 percent of their sales to developed Europe and just 13.7 percent to emerging markets. On the opposite side of the spectrum one found the mega caps, which made up the top 40 percent of MSCI Europe market capitalization. In 2007 they sold 23.8 percent to emerging markets,

Table 6.1 Revenue Exposure, 2007 by Industry Group

Industry Group	Developed Europe	Emerging Europe*	Middle East & Africa	Asia	North America	Latin America	Emerging Markets†
Automobiles & Components	56.6	6.7	4.2	10.4	14.6	7.4	26.8
Banks	71.3	4.8	1.6	8.1	9.0	5.2	19.4
Capital Goods	55.6	6.4	4.4	11.4	18.8	3.4	24.4
Commercial Services & Supply	70.8	2.0	1.2	6.3	17.7	2.1	9.3
Consumer Durables & Apparel	47.5	5.2	1.8	17.4	23.8	4.2	23.1
Consumer Services	81.1	0.1	0.7	3.3	13.7	1.2	4.6
Diversified Financials	56.0	1.4	0.1	9.0	29.6	3.9	11.9
Energy	56.2	10.2	6.8	5.3	16.7	4.7	27.1
Food & Staples Retailing	73.0	9.0	0.3	5.2	8.9	3.6	18.0
Food Beverage & Tobacco	40.6	9.9	6.0	11.3	21.5	10.6	36.2
Health Care Equipment & Services	42.6	1.4	0.0	7.5	45.5	3.0	9.0
Household & Personal Products	47.1	7.8	2.5	9.4	28.1	5.2	22.8
Insurance	67.7	3.7	2.5	6.2	18.3	1.6	12.8
Materials	45.9	9.3	4.5	14.4	19.9	6.1	32.1
Media	66.1	1.5	2.4	5.5	23.5	1.0	10.0
Pharmaceuticals Bio & Life Sc.	33.1	2.4	2.1	11.4	47.3	3.7	14.1
Real Estate	93.7	5.8	0.0	0.0	0.5	0.0	5.8
Retailing	85.6	2.2	2.5	4.5	4.1	1.1	9.4
Semiconductors	30.3	0.0	0.9	48.2	20.6	0.0	44.6
Software & Services	73.9	0.7	1.0	5.6	17.0	1.9	7.4
Technology Hardware & Equi.	27.6	12.6	13.2	27.6	10.4	8.5	61.3
Telecommunication Services	79.7	4.5	0.9	1.7	5.1	8.2	15.2
Transportation	65.7	6.0	2.9	8.9	12.2	4.4	20.0
Utilities	83.8	4.5	0.5	1.1	5.8	4.3	10.4
MSCI Europe	61.8	6.3	3.3	7.9	15.9	4.8	21.2

Notes: Data refer to 2007 estimates and are based on company information combined with Morgan Stanley's estimates.

*Emerging Europe includes Eastern Europe, Russia, and the former Soviet Union.

†Emerging markets are here defined as the world ex the United States, Canada, developed Europe, and Japan.

Source: Morgan Stanley, reproduced with permission.

Table 8.2 Comparing Industry Group Revenue Exposure in 2004 and 2007

Industry Group	Developed Europe Exposure (%) 2004	2007e	North America Exposure (%) 2004	2007e	EM Exposure (%) 2004	2007e	Change in Exposure Dev. Eur.	N. A.	EM†
Automobiles & Components	56.8	56.6	24.1	14.6	18.0	26.8	-0.2	-9.4	8.7
Banks	76.8	71.3	9.4	9.0	13.3	19.4	-5.4	-0.4	6.2
Capital Goods	56.6	55.6	21.8	18.8	20.1	24.4	-1.0	-3.0	4.3
Commercial Services & Supply	68.6	70.8	20.3	17.7	8.2	9.3	2.2	-2.6	1.1
Consumer Durables & Apparel	59.1	47.5	25.3	23.8	11.9	23.1	-11.5	-1.5	11.2
Consumer Services	75.2	81.1	18.3	13.7	5.6	4.6	5.9	-4.6	-1.0
Diversified Financials	61.2	56.0	25.2	29.6	12.5	11.9	-5.2	4.4	-0.6
Energy	53.1	56.2	22.9	16.7	24.0	27.1	3.1	-6.2	3.1
Food & Staples Retailing	72.9	73.0	14.8	8.9	12.1	18.0	0.1	-5.9	5.9
Food Beverage & Tobacco	40.8	40.6	22.9	21.5	34.3	36.2	-0.2	-1.3	2.0
Health Care Equipment & Services	41.8	42.6	44.6	45.5	9.7	9.0	0.8	0.8	-0.7
Household & Personal Products	54.2	47.1	22.8	28.1	20.5	22.8	-7.2	5.2	2.4
Insurance	75.2	67.7	16.9	18.3	5.9	12.8	-7.4	1.4	6.9
Materials	52.8	45.9	18.2	19.9	25.7	32.1	-6.9	1.7	6.4
Media	72.4	66.1	18.5	23.5	7.8	10.0	-6.2	5.0	2.1
Pharmaceuticals Bio & Life Sc.	34.2	33.1	41.3	47.3	17.0	14.1	-1.1	5.9	-2.9
Real Estate	98.9	93.7	1.1	0.5	0.0	5.8	-5.2	-0.6	5.8
Retailing	90.9	85.6	4.8	4.1	4.0	9.4	-5.4	-0.7	5.4
Semiconductors	29.9	30.3	18.4	20.6	46.9	44.6	0.4	2.2	-2.3
Software & Services	76.5	73.9	18.1	17.0	5.4	7.4	-2.6	-1.2	2.0
Technology Hardware & Equi.	34.4	27.6	12.8	10.4	51.3	61.3	-6.7	-2.4	9.9
Telecommunication Services	79.9	79.7	6.1	5.1	12.0	15.2	-0.1	-1.0	3.2
Transportation	72.6	65.7	12.4	12.2	13.6	20.0	-6.8	-0.2	6.5
Utilities	85.2	83.8	5.3	5.8	9.4	10.4	-1.4	0.5	1.0
MSCI Europe	64.9	61.8	17.6	15.9	16.1	21.2	-3.0	-1.8	5.1

Notes: Data refer to 2007 estimates and are based on company information combined with Morgan Stanley's estimates.
† Emerging markets defined as the world ex the United States, Canada, developed Europe, and Japan.

18.2 percent to North America and 56.7 percent to developed Europe.

When it comes to corporate Europe, both Morgan Stanley's statistics and trade-flow data confirm a declining role for the United States as a major source of business; we therefore argue that a strong bull market in the Old Continent can easily coexist with a faltering dollar, as happened in 2003–2007 (although contrary to long-term experience). Of course, this does not mean that dollar movements are irrelevant in the struggle for economic existence and success. Estimates are that a 10-percent fall of the dollar is matched by a 3-percent fall in European earnings.[7] The more vulnerable sectors are usually energy, autos, materials, utilities, and capital goods, while luxury goods, machinery, and textile apparel—with a large exposure to Asia—may respond negatively to a weak yen.

Investors should also consider that Eurozone companies have accustomed themselves to living with a strong euro. Therefore, if—contrary to our expectations—the common currency enters a bear market, the lower exchange rate will relax pricing pressure on the tradable sector and the benefits will go straight to the bottom line of corporate Europe.

Petrodollars and Europe

If the authors' stance is correct that a primary downward trend for the dollar is not yet over, it is also worth analyzing how expensive commodity prices can influence business, considering that high commodity prices are often the mirror image of a shaky dollar. What is the possible fallout for corporate Europe vis-à-vis corporate America? We are not speaking of commodity-related companies here, since the answer is obvious in their case. But we do want to know where commodity-rich countries spend their additional revenue. And it seems that Europe is a better place than the United States in this regard. Say it depends on the fact that the sheiks love Ferraris, French fashion, or German supercars more than American merchandise. Or say it is the political dislike of the Russians toward their old enemy, but more petrodollars find their way into Europe than into the United States.

The Organization for Economic Cooperation and Development offered an eye-opening study in its *Economic Outlook* of June 2008, titled "The Respending of Oil Revenues in OECD Economies" (see Figures 8.2 and 8.3). According to the study, the external demand

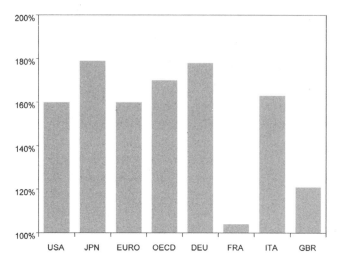

Figure 8.2   How Oil Producers Respend Their Petrodollars in OECD Countries—Increase in Exports to Oil Producers, 2002–2007
Source: OECD, *Economic Outlook,* June 2008.

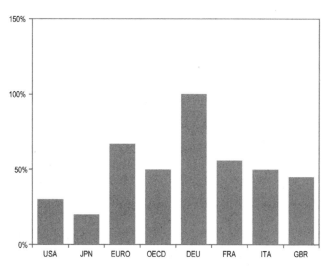

Figure 8.3   Oil Producers Love the Eurozone
Note: Additional exports to oil producers per additional imports from oil producers, accumulated 2002–2007.
Source: OECD, *Economic Outlook,* June 2008.

emanating from oil producers (OPEC, Russia, and Norway) had a stimulating effect on OECD-area exports.

Higher oil prices enhanced oil producers' disposable income, and the additional purchasing power augmented OECD exports to these economies by 170 percent in 2002–2007. The United States and the Eurozone enjoyed similar figures, both about 150 percent. Yet, the respending rate by oil producers was vastly different: Of euro-area additional payments for oil imports accumulated between 2002 and 2007, about two-thirds came back in the form of additional exports to oil-producing countries. In the case of Germany, the extra amount of money spent on the oil bill was fully met by an equally increased volume of exports to the same oil producers. By contrast, only 30 percent of the supplementary oil bill paid by the United States was respent in the purchase of U.S. merchandise. To prove that Europe is second to none when it comes to exports, the corresponding ratio for Japan was even more meager, that is, 20 percent.

Regarding the oil-rich countries, there may be a strong inducement for them to buy stocks, unless commodity prices do not suffer a major collapse. If one divides the price of oil by the global stock market price/earnings, the number obtained is a measure of the buying power of oil barrels to corporate earnings. The higher the number, the greater the corporate earnings a barrel of oil can buy. In the summer of 2009 this ratio was much higher than in the 1990s. So, what could be better for oil producers than to diversify their assets, exchanging barrels of oil for depressed corporate earnings? Again, the trend should be global and lift worldwide stocks, but even more so Eurozone ones, if we are right that the common-currency area offers a discount to the United States.

PART III

THE GURU CHAPTERS

CHAPTER 9

When It Is America That Diversifies Out of the Dollar

AN INTERVIEW WITH WILLIAM CLARK

I happened to meet William Clark at a conference in Paris on May 13, 2008—it was a flash in the dark, and I shall explain why.[1] As a journalist covering financial markets, I perfectly understood the discomfort of the central banks in newly industrialized countries: They were sitting on and continuing to raise large amounts of reserves denominated in a weakening currency, namely the greenback. It was also clear to any observer that a persistent and ever-growing decline of the dollar was not something foreign investors loved to live with. But William Clark introduced a new element: It was the American managers who started to diversify out of U.S. assets, because they were concerned about the inflationary aspects of a falling dollar. Clark was talking from personal experience. Since March 2005, he has directed the investment operations of the State of New Jersey pension fund, that is to say, one of the nation's 15 largest public funds, providing retirement benefits to more than 780,000 current and future public retirees. Total assets under management were over \$65 bn at the time of this interview (August 2009).

But let's go back to Paris for a moment. Clark spelled out how he had been changing the composition of his portfolio in response to a depreciating dollar and the inflationary dynamics that could spring from it. He had been in the process of lowering the exposure to U.S. stocks, while increasing the weight of overseas bourses. And he had embarked on a series of maneuvers to counteract price pressures. To illustrate: Commodities, real estate, and Treasury inflation-protected securities had made their entry into the New Jersey pension fund's portfolio. It was a radical shift, since, in 2005, the fund had zero exposure to commodities, zero exposure to inflation-protected securities, and was a much more domestically oriented actor.

Clark then showed a revelatory slide, describing how the whole pension fund industry was moving and positioning itself in a similar vein (see also the chapter on valuation); that is, it was diversifying, and diversifying out of the dollar.

Clark's interview reveals how a weak dollar can play a causal role in encouraging U.S. holders of assets lo look abroad. It should also highlight the interplay between U.S. policies and market expectations: If confidence is shaken in the purchasing power of the dollar, it may not be China that disgorges U.S. assets but also many U.S. investors.

How do Eurozone stocks enter the story? When we talked in Paris, Clark was significantly overweighting the Old Continent in connection with his overall strategy of diversification abroad. Then, during the crash of 2008, he retreated and went underweight. It will be remembered from Chapter 7 that this was a common pattern among global managers and was reflected in Bank of America–Merrill Lynch's surveys.

Now some good news for the Eurozone: Clark is planning to return toward an overweighting presence in the Old Continent. His words offer an inside look into the decision-making process of a large U.S. institutional manager struggling with the challenges associated with a weak dollar.

Vincenzo Sciarretta: Mr. Clark, would you provide us with a retrospective analysis of what happened in the U.S. pension fund industry during the crisis of late 2008 and early 2009?

William Clark: The pension fund industry endured a big liquidity squeeze. A lot of players were making large commitments to private equity, real estate, and hedge funds to try and diversify their portfolios.[2] Now, the way these investments work is roughly the following: You make a commitment, and then, over time (normally two to three years), when the fund finds some opportunities, they call your money in. This money remains invested over the fund's "investment period," normally seven to ten years. And you can't sell the investment, or it is very, very difficult to do so. Pension funds committed an awful lot of money into these vehicles. Then, when the crash hit, they could not dismantle their private equity positions. On the contrary, there was a continuing investment to be made here because the private equity funds kept on calling the money in.

Sciarretta: So what?

Clark: So many pension funds went through a painful liquidity squeeze. Normally, they would be buyers in the course of a decline, but in this episode, most of them were forced sellers at the low point. That tells part of the story.

Sciarretta: And you?

Clark: I think we were lucky enough to avoid the worst scenario. Although, on a modest scale, we bought some additional stocks in the fall of 2008, which turned out to be okay. But the biggest position we took was in U.S. corporate bonds, and it worked really well. [They sharply rebounded afterward.] Now we have been selling corporate bonds and we have been moving into equity markets.

Sciarretta: At the time of the conference in Paris—May 2008—you argued that the dollar was vulnerable, and this rendered U.S. assets less attractive than usual. What about now?

Clark: I am even more concerned now than then.

Sciarretta: Because the dollar is still likely to depreciate?

Clark: Yes. It has to depreciate. Not in a straight line, but the path of least resistance leads to a weaker dollar. We Americans are counting on foreign central banks to keep us afloat. The risk is that when the level of economic growth picks up, foreigners decide to opt for more attractive alternatives rather than buying U.S. Treasuries at current interest rates.

Sciarretta: Are you still enlarging your presence in foreign equity markets?

Clark: Yes, I am. As an order of magnitude, I would say that now our stock benchmark is half domestic and half international. A couple of years ago it would have been two-thirds U.S. and one-third international. We have been gradually shifting out of the dollar. I believe that most U.S. pensions are doing the same thing.

Sciarretta: It seems that the dollar's fall is largely affecting your decision process.

Clark: I would say so. Another concern of mine is that a weak currency may inexorably encourage inflation. The risk is palpable and requires some countermeasures.

Sciarretta: For instance?

Clark: We have established a large allocation in inflation-protected securities. It's big money: $3.4 bn, or about 5 percent of the portfolio. Once we had nothing there; we were in non-inflation index bonds. Likewise, we have a commodity allocation of 3 percent, because if you predict a gradual depreciation of the dollar, commodities are an obvious beneficiary.

Sciarretta: Again on stocks: Do you expect to keep on augmenting the exposure to overseas markets?

Clark: Yes. [His answer was quick and resolute.] Both in Europe and in other areas, particularly emerging markets. We pay great attention to newly industrialized markets.

Sciarretta: You said you have been enlarging the presence abroad, including Europe. Do you believe this is a general tendency across the whole U.S. pension fund industry?

Clark: Yes, I believe so.

Sciarretta: Also for the future?

Clark: Yes. My impression is that many funds are considering benchmarking against more globally exposed indexes, such as the MSCI World.

Sciarretta: In May 2008 you had a strong position in continental Europe; then you cut back during the crisis, and now you are rebuilding your presence. What's the next move?

Clark: Ultimately, assuming a normal growth cycle, I think we'll go back more heavily into Europe. I don't want the single currency to be too strong, because it hurts exports, but we are pretty confident that the euro will fare well compared to the dollar. From a long-term perspective, we'll probably continue to increase our exposure to Europe.

Sciarretta: Many analysts explain why the dollar is vulnerable, yet a traveler could answer back that a European city like Paris is more expensive than most U.S. cities. Shouldn't this lean in favor of the U.S. currency?

Clark: I agree that a cheap currency may attract an influx of foreign capital to acquire attractive U.S. assets. But I do not think it's enough. The dollar is likely to continue along its gradual descent, simply because nothing has changed that can induce a trend reversal. I am not calling for a catastrophic drop in the dollar—nothing like a 30 percent devaluation. Just a gradual descent.

Sciarretta: When you decide to buy Eurozone stocks, what are your guidelines?

Clark: We do not index. We have a small, devoted team and manage our European portfolio very actively. I would say it is more sector allocation than country allocation, but obviously you look at both.

Sciarretta: Can you focus on any sector you like more in the Eurozone than in the United States?

Clark: I like consumer-product companies. Eurozone consumers are in much better shape than their American peers. At least, they have generous savings rates to start with, whereas American households are overextended. Another good sector is heath care, since it ought to benefit from the aging population, and the businesses have good fundamentals.

Sciarretta: On the other hand, what don't you like?

Clark: We try to avoid companies that may react negatively to a shock in Eastern Europe. For instance, we have been concerned about the Nordic banking sector, given its large exposure to the Baltics. That's a country risk we have been very focused on. I am aware that others disagree, but we are still cautious about Eastern European areas that borrowed markedly in foreign currencies, such as Hungary or the Baltics.

10

Yes, Europe Is Cheaper than the United States (and the Gap Is Not Justified any Longer)

AN INTERVIEW WITH FELIX ZULAUF

I expect European equities to outperform U.S. equities," says Felix Zulauf, president and founder of Zulauf Asset Management, based in Zug, Switzerland. He warns that Anglo-Saxon consumers are strangulated by an unparalleled level of debt and, going forward, he doubts that "Wall Street deserves a large premium any longer." Eurozone stocks, for their part, reached a deep low in March 2009, which may very well constitute a generational low in valuations: From that point onward, patient investors should make money.

Felix Zulauf is well-known as a member of *Barron's* magazine roundtable, where he has been a participant for over 20 years. In 2008, the Swiss manager confessed a bearish posture on equity markets, declaring to *Barron's* readers that selling short consumer discretionary stocks and European auto producers could be a good idea, because the global economy was entering a severe recession—and he was right. He was also right that the pound sterling was an easy short, while gold was an attractive long.

In March 2009, he called for a sharp rebound of equity indexes, although, as he explains in this interview, the long-term bear market is not necessarily over.

Zulauf is the kind of manager who approaches investment challenges from a macro standpoint and comfortably engages assets as various as cotton or sugar on one hand and European blue chips on the other.

Born in 1950, Zulauf worked for several leading investment banks in New York, Zurich, and Paris. Then, in 1990, he founded a wholly owned firm, Zulauf Asset Management AG, assuring him the freedom to pursue his own investment style. The company was in transition during the first part of this decade and from 2003 Zulauf acted as advisor only. Finally, in spring 2009, Zulauf Asset Management was split into two parts, and Felix Zulauf now fully owns the split-off Zulauf Asset Management AG, which focuses on managing a conservative global macro fund, as well as on offering advisory services to selected family offices and institutions. In this interview, Zulauf explains why the Eurozone is cheaper than the United States and where some real investment opportunities are.

Vincenzo Sciarretta:	Mr. Zulauf, was March 2009 a generational low for Western stock markets?
Felix Zulauf:	I would distinguish between the Eurozone and the United States. The selling apex of September 2008 to March 2009 led the Old Continent stock markets to an extreme that I would deem as not incongruous with a secular low. Stocks, on average, were changing hands at about book value, and dividend yields were exceeding 5 percent—an attractive combination going forward 10 years or so. You should make money based on those valuations.
Sciarretta:	What about the United States?
Zulauf:	Stock indexes never came down that far. The lowest point was about 1.5 times book value, and dividend yield was around 3.7 percent. That's not enough, in my opinion. I guess March 2009 marked a cyclical extreme but not the ultimate bottom for valuations.
Sciarretta:	Why do you say so?
Zulauf:	Because valuations in equity markets move from one extreme to the other and never-ever reverse midway, going back to the previous extreme. That means a pendulum that swings from deep undervaluation to eventual deep overvaluation and all the way back to deep undervaluation. The cycle can last, say, 20 years on one side, or could be shorter, 10 to 15 years. Obviously,

when you buy at high valuations, your future returns will be low, and when you buy at low valuations your returns will be high. Accordingly, it is very important for long-term investors to buy at the right point in time.

Sciarretta: Do you expect Wall Street to drop and eventually touch fresh lows?

Zulauf: It may be. Or it may be the passage of time that drives valuations down. However, sometime in 2010–2012— during the next downleg—U.S. stock multiples are likely to decline further and ultimately reach the point we have seen in Europe. If my analysis is correct, investors should wait a few additional years before taking a truly optimistic stance for the long run.

Sciarretta: Why are valuations lower on the European side of the Atlantic?

Zulauf: I guess part of the story is related to the old assessment that America showed greater economic dynamism than Europe; hence market participants were willing to pay a somewhat richer price for U.S. stocks. This assertion may prove to be false in the future. The United States will be laboring under unfavorable conditions of debt, and could languish with high unemployment and little growth. Like Europe, or probably even worse. I doubt Wall Street deserves a large premium any longer; its stock market may have to adjust to the downside.

Sciarretta: Are you implying the adjustment is yet to come?

Zulauf: Right. I would think that during the next five years—my guess is in two or three years—we will see the final low. I don't know where to put such a low, but I believe it will be associated with lower valuations for the United States vis-à-vis the March 2009 low. Meanwhile, Europe could come back to roughly the same level as in March 2009. At that point, it will be time to play the stock market with greater conviction.

Sciarretta: While, in the interim, you see greater risk for the United States than for the Eurozone, don't you?

Zulauf: Yes, I do. On a relative basis, I expect European equities to outperform U.S. equities.

Sciarretta: Going back to Europe, you mentioned that dividends were attractive against bond interests.

Zulauf:	Yes, some industrial blue chips offer dividend yields well in excess of five-year bonds. Moreover, the payout ratio [the percentage of earnings the shareholder gets in the form of dividends] is often below 60 percent and therefore sustainable going forward.

It's the first time in the last 20 years that dividends are so rewarding versus government obligations. From a long-term perspective, I'd say that, compared to bonds, stocks were never as attractive as they are now; and were even more so in March 2009. In the United States, as an example, the total return of equities versus government bonds had deviated on the downside from its mean since 1926 by three standard deviations. The last time the reading was that extreme was in 1932 at the Depression low. That is about as good as it gets.

Sciarretta: Would you mention a few names to help us understand which stocks you are referring to?

Zulauf: I am referring primarily to giants in the energy group: companies such as ENI, Total, or Royal Dutch. In telecoms I would look at Deutsche Telecom or Swisscom. And you find good opportunities among utilities as well, for instance, E.ON in Germany.

Sciarretta: In reading your comments and interviews, you seem especially worried about the distress in the household sector and the unraveling of credit.

Zulauf: That's true. We are in the early stages of a deleveraging process that will last for years and throw a negative light on consumer spending, economic activity, and equity markets. In 2009, unprecedented expansionary policies counterbalanced the reduced role of consumers. In other words, the deleveraging of the private sector was mirrored by the rapid leveraging of the public sector. But at some point, the contraction in credit will come back to haunt us. Consumers are still on the ropes; it will take years for them to regain financial health.

Sciarretta: Are you contemplating the possibility of selling the stock market short?

Zulauf: Yes, absolutely. I operate on the assumption that we are in a secular bear market and I intend to sell short as soon as the uptrend runs out of steam.

Sciarretta: You mentioned that households are overextended and need to tighten their belts because the credit bubble is deflating. However, one could argue that the situation is much different in the Eurozone, where household savings rates are often greater than 10 percent, and sometimes close to 15 percent. In the United States, it's just a few percentage points.

Zulauf: I agree that savings rates in the Eurozone are much higher than in the United States. But in some cases, the Eurozone consumer is also leveraged, in particular against home prices. In Spain or Ireland—to name a few hot potatoes—real estate followed an Anglo-Saxon boom-burst sequence. The only country that was untouched is Germany, where house prices have been apathetic for decades. Germany has structural problems, but virtually no cyclical imbalances.

Sciarretta: Some claim that if Germany still had the Deutsche mark, it would now see its currency going definitely up.

Zulauf: You got it. Germany was overpriced entering the Monetary Union; the European partners were cautious and a little bit circumspect about Germany's reunification; they wanted it to happen only within a larger Europe. Further, especially the French advocated Berlin's entry into the Monetary Union at a high exchange rate, so as to prevent the new Germany from becoming exceedingly dominant through the export channel. That's my theory, at least. Berlin had to deflate and catch up, because it had the wrong exchange rate to start with. Unit labor costs have been declining for years against neighbors' equivalent figures. Real estate never moved up. Consumer credit remained within the constraints of prudence. Germany is once again underpriced and appears as the most competitive player around. The export position continues to be satisfactory. If Berlin had its own currency, no doubt it would go up.

Sciarretta: If it comes to a choice, would you overweight German assets within the Eurozone?

Zulauf: Yes, I would. German companies—mark my words—are very competitive within the Eurozone and should

	perform accordingly. Moreover, China's rise means persistent demand for high-quality machinery, where Germany is the world champion. You want to be positioned to sell the Chinese what they need and not to compete with them in low-quality consumer goods.
Sciarretta:	And as regards real estate?
Zulauf:	Along with Japan and Switzerland, Germany's housing market did not have a boom. Indeed, Germany had no credit boom, no mortgage boom, and no real estate boom. Residential prices are the same as 15 years ago. My feeling: If you buy a market that has not boomed, your future returns ought to be superior to areas that already went through the roof and are now in the process of deflating.
Sciarretta:	Let's return to the deleveraging process. How healthy is the balance sheet of corporate Europe?
Zulauf:	On the whole, corporate Europe is more leveraged than corporate America.[1] In the old days, the scenario was different. Europeans used to be much more conservative than the Anglo-Saxons, but as the latter received higher returns on equity, and since gearing became almost a synonym of dynamism, the new generation of managers went on a debt binge. However, from here on, users of credit will try to limit their exposure or cut it back all around.
Sciarretta:	And banks are also on shaky ground.
Zulauf:	Many Eurozone banks are more leveraged than their U.S. counterparts. That's a problem. It means that growth must be financed within tight lending targets. I would say that if in the United States the consumer is facing borrowing constraints, in Europe you have far more lending constraints by the banking industry.
Sciarretta:	Do you linger over any other risks?
Zulauf:	I am not optimistic about the prospects of Eastern Europe for some time to come. Countries such as Hungary, Romania, and Slovakia have lived beyond their means. Consumer spending was prodigal. External deficits skyrocketed. The countries relied on capital inflows, but the capital inflows are now gone.
	In recent years, you could develop the argument that there was a movement of Eastern Europe toward

Western Europe. Now Eastern Europe is sending a shockwave westward. That's bad, because Eastern Europe depends to a large extent on Western Europe in terms of export, financing, and the like. It's an uncomfortable position to be in.

Sciarretta: Yes, but those markets collapsed almost to the vanishing point. Do you think the problems are reflected in asset prices or not?

Zulauf: I honestly must say that we are not investing in Eastern Europe, because we do not trust those markets, and they are not so liquid. I have invested in Russia in the past, but I think Russia created another problem when it reclaimed rights from foreign companies in natural resources. That was a major mistake that will be detrimental when Russia tries to attract new technology and financing to recover its natural resources.

Sciarretta: But, again, the bullish argument is that Russian stocks tanked 90 percent, top to bottom.

Zulauf: I do not exclude that if we have a commodity boom, you can successfully participate in the Russian stock market. For instance, you may consider major blue chips for a while, but I would not look at that as a long-term investment, because the legal framework is not trustworthy.

Sciarretta: Let me change the subject: We have talked about the euro area and Eastern Europe. You were rather confident that a secular low for the former was reached in March 2009. By contrast, you showed pessimism on Eastern Europe. My next question: What about the United Kingdom? Some underline that the UK is enduring a combination of problems similar to those of the United States, but to the nth power: namely, too much finance, too much consumer spending and leverage, too big a housing bubble. Others answer that all the aforementioned problems are real, but since both UK stocks and the UK currency plummeted in 2008, prices look so depressed as to be attractive. Do you have an opinion?

Zulauf: Both theses are correct; it is a question of timing. To start with, pound weakness is likely to bring relief to the exporting sectors, which help the UK economy in the short run. But medium-term I am rather pessimistic. Consumers have been lulled into a false sense of security. They are in an even more precarious position than U.S. consumers and have not begun to adjust their behavior. After a few quarters of rebound, I guess the UK will begin to suffer again, because credit shrinkage has gloomy consequences for the economy, withdrawing resources from consumption and investment. At that point, economic activity will undershoot expectations, and the UK currency will become vulnerable to a greater fall.

Sciarretta: What about the euro?

Zulauf: We often pit the euro against the dollar. And the dollar is on a secular decline, which follows the relative decline of the United States as a nation, as an economic power. The United States is still big, still dominating, but on a relative decline. Former reserve currencies had a long way to fall when they entered their descending phase; so, from that angle, a strong euro is the mirror image of a weak dollar. There will be cyclical rallies for the U.S. currency. The rallies usually come when liquidity tightens or when deflationary forces shake investor confidence. Hence, if my prediction is true that sometime in 2010–2012 we will have a new bear leg in the stock markets, the dollar may go up; but it's a rally, it's temporary. Otherwise, I would not recommend Europeans to put their money into U.S. dollars.

Sciarretta: But reportedly, you question the very existence of the euro in the long haul.

Zulauf: I say the euro is an experiment in progress that needs to be kept under observation, because previous attempts to form a monetary union on the Continent failed to survive the test of time.

Sciarretta: Where could the pressure come from?

Zulauf: The single currency combines several structurally different economies and forces them into a single monetary policy, a single interest rate. When deflationary tendencies emerge, the union is shaken to its foundations, since the traditional mechanisms to relieve pressure are not available any longer. In normal circumstances, countries with a large current-account deficit—like Spain—would devalue by 20 or 30 percent, and that would be the main avenue to counteract a deflationary spiral. Yet, in the present setting, the exchange rate is unavailable. What's left? Politicians would plead for transfer payments, which involve a deep intermediation of European authorities, and in consequence are highly regarded by the same authorities.

Sciarretta: Could it work?

Zulauf: I doubt it. Most of the running would have to be done by the Germans, yet the Germans are not prepared to increase their burden of payments to other member countries—they themselves are financially under pressure. This means the adjustment must hit the real economy. In a deflationary spiral, jobs are decimated and the real question becomes how much pain those economies can stand before the political landscape begins to change and some influential political parties call for an exit strategy from the euro.

Sciarretta: But the exit strategy would be immensely expensive.

Zulauf: Well, if you play according to the rules. But if things get bad enough, governments will behave according to their best short-term interests, and not in observance of the laws.

Sciarretta: I am not speaking of the laws here, but rather of the economic consequences of exiting the euro: You have to change the banking system, the accounting system, the payment system, the pinball machines of the kids, and the cigarette dispensers of the parents—in short, everything. Further, can you imagine the hit on the markets?

Zulauf: I understand, but in the worst-case scenario, do you really want 30 percent unemployment, or are you going to reintroduce the peseta, the lira, the drachma?

Sciarretta: I guess that if you are on the verge of an economic collapse, and you exit the euro, your economy will instantly collapse to the vanishing point, and this long before any pick-up can even remotely take place. Further, I do not see the political willingness to retreat from the euro. One could argue that in 2009 California had huge fiscal problems, but nobody yelled, "Let's abandon the dollar!" Why should it happen in the Eurozone?

Zulauf: No, the two sets of circumstances are really different. The formation of the United States was an enlarging process, from one state to the next, over a long period of time. And—to be honest—they fought wars along the way. Then there's another difference: Let's say that high oil prices precipitate a recession in the automobile-producing area of Detroit. People can still move to Texas or another region that's doing well. After all, it's the same nation, the same language, the same legal framework, same schools, same culture—it's easy. But do you really think the guy from southern Italy will move to Finland?

Sciarretta: Well, I don't know about Finland, but there are lots of Italians in every corner of the world. However, I do agree that language differences within the Eurozone represent a strong barrier to internal mobility.

Zulauf: Another fear of mine: If member-state economies begin to diverge, the ultimate result of the European integration might be the European disintegration, as rising nationalism gains momentum.

Sciarretta: I do hope you are wrong. I am 40, and my generation is the first not to experience a war on the Continent. We often fail to recognize the huge political successes of the European Union: Instead of millions of corpses, the European nations have been experiencing a long period of peace and prosperity. We must be grateful and hope the tide will not turn. But now, let's stop the political digression and go back to the investment framework. If you do not consider the 2008 crisis finished, what's the next step?

Zulauf: We risked a systemic implosion; we saw the abyss falling away at our feet. The governments and the central banks came in, providing not only help but all sorts of stimuli. We have witnessed the greatest market manipulation of modern times. It buys time; it buys at least one year. The authorities flooded the markets with a combination of liquidity and stimuli, which sparked a strong recovery. I don't know how far the revival of the financial markets will go, but probably not as far as many think. The economy and the markets are greatly dependent on the government measures, and when the band-aids are removed, we are back to the crux of the matter: How do we cope with the deleveraging wave?

You have to realize that the U.S. economy and a few others are in a balance sheet recession. That is when indebted economic subjects change their focus from maximizing profits to minimizing debt. The result will be debt repayment and bankruptcies. One needs to understand that savings used to repay debt are lost from our system and the effect is that the private economy shrinks as a result. The public sector has to compensate this. But with government indebtedness exploding, there will be a political backlash and stimuli will be withdrawn once the politicians feel the economy is on its own foot again. Then we will most likely see a relapse into recession again.

Sciarretta: If you are right, and stocks go down worldwide, when should investors expect the final bottom?

Zulauf: Probably in 2011–2012.

Sciarretta: Okay, what about sectors in the Eurozone stock market that, under any reasonable scenario, have a good chance to outperform the averages? Any sectors an investor might buy against the overall market?

Zulauf: For a dynamic portfolio, an investor needs to own technology, industrials, and maybe insurance on the way up. However, in my view, the structural set-up is for a continuing rise of the emerging economies and that's why I believe that the back-end groups (energy, infrastructure, selected capital goods, and mining) are the structural leaders. This is very different from previous cycles. They will also have another downturn once the economy relapses, but, this notwithstanding, they are likely to lead for several years as they benefit the most from the structural rise and industrialization of China and the like. That's how I would play it.

Sciarretta: Can you cite a few stock names you like?

Zulauf: I am not a stock picker, really. However, I would buy some energy companies that are inexpensive and have good prospects, such as Total or ENI. I would hold some gold—which is not specific to Europe, but I would definitely hold gold. BHP Billiton or any other leading mining company should be a good choice, as could be a capital goods company like ABB. For the more defensive part, I would buy some utilities, like Germany's E.On. And I would stay with short-term bonds—nothing longer than three to four years.

Sciarretta: What could a long-term investor do?

Zulauf: My recommendation would be the following: Since the early 1980s, interest rates have declined a long way and now are close to the end of that movement. This is especially true for government bond yields. They are forming a secular bottom, and the bottoming out may need another few years to be completed. Deflationary forces are strong, but government policies carry with them the seeds of inflation. In this phase, I would want to be a prudent investor, and above all I would want to preserve my wealth. The core portfolio would consist of bonds with maturities of maybe three or four years, not longer, as I mentioned. A more aggressive investor should include some of the stocks mentioned before. Then, sometime in 2011–2012, I would switch from bonds to stocks, preferring companies that cater to the Chinese and participate in the rise of that economy as well as those of other emerging economies. Capital goods, infrastructure, and mining will most likely be among the best performers. I would also buy classic blue chips with good balance sheets, deeply rooted in the basic necessities of the consumer, and with an intact business model (such as energy, utilities, telecommunications, or personal household goods). I would want stocks with high dividend yields, payout ratios well below 60 percent, and a price-to-earnings ratio not exceeding 10. If the next downleg is severe—as I think it will be—we may be lucky enough to find companies whose dividend yields are higher than their price-to-earnings ratios and are therefore very attractive for the long term. That would be my portfolio construction.

CHAPTER 11

Europe–Asia: The Promising Linkage

AN INTERVIEW WITH MARC FABER

W hen it comes to analyzing investments in developing nations, Marc Faber is second to none. So I was extremely delighted when he accepted our request to discuss the interactions among Europe, emerging countries, and the United States. It would have been difficult to find a more qualified person.

Faber's official biography tells us that he was born in Zurich, Switzerland, went to school in Geneva, and studied economics at the University of Zurich (although the young man often preferred skiing to lessons). After a PhD magna cum laude, Faber began working at Drexel Burnham Lambert, when the firm was the junk-bond king of Wall Street. In 1973 he moved to Asia, lived a quarter of a century in Hong Kong, and in 2000 made Chiangmai, in northern Thailand, his new home.

Faber publishes a monthly investment newsletter, *The Gloom Boom & Doom Report*,[1] universally known in the financial community. It is a bulletin that aims at discovering unusual investment opportunities and covers, above all, emerging markets, Wall Street, and commodities.

The media portrays Marc Faber as an engaging personality and an accomplished human being who lives exactly the life he wants to be living. Journalists often exalt him as a guru, a prophet of our time, for his numerous successful calls, or as a travelling oracle, for his countless trips around the globe, giving speeches, meeting clients, searching out the last investment gem, or just spending a few hours in a nightclub or disco. Faber operates as an investment advisor and fund manager through Marc Faber Limited.

He has also been nicknamed Dr. Doom, for his tendency to predict disasters: In 1987 he warned clients to cash out before Black Monday. In 2000 he was very confident that the Nasdaq would drop by at least 70 percent. In 2005–2006 he wrote at length about the impending crash of home prices. Yet, labeling Faber as Dr. Doom is in part unfair, since he has proved to be a great market visionary on the long side as well. In March 2009 he announced a sharp rally in stocks. In 1998–1999 he made a strong case in favor of gold. After the Nasdaq tumble, he assumed a bullish stance on commodities and emerging markets.

Vincenzo Sciarretta:	Dr. Faber, politically, how do you see the relationship among China, Europe, and the United States?
Marc Faber:	One point is clear to me: China is emerging as a leading economic power and, over time, will exert a formidable influence not only in Southeast and Central Asia but all over the world. Therefore, Beijing won't abide being pushed around by other countries. First of all at home, Sino politicians will become more and more uneasy about the presence of U.S. military bases to the south, in the Pacific, and also on its western border, namely in Central Asia. I envision the possibility of growing tensions between China and the United States, and I wonder how Washington will react to Beijing's ascendant role.
Sciarretta:	What's your personal answer?
Faber:	The future is nebulous, of course. But the one thing I do know is that shifts in the international distribution of power can lead to frictions and—in many cases—to military confrontation.
Sciarretta:	How do you put Europe in the picture?
Faber:	In general, I think that Asians—disliking the foreign policy of the United States and not trusting the United States in any way—are more likely to be increasingly involved with Europe, also because they recognize the Old Continent is a huge market, larger than the United States in many respects.
Sciarretta:	Is there any particular stock market sector where Europe has a clear advantage over America?

Faber:	I would bet on luxury goods manufacturers, including high-end cars. It is not unfair to say that one of the problems of the United States is that its industries do not really have the products the Asians want.
Sciarretta:	What are you speaking of?
Faber:	Listen: When Asians become wealthier, the first thing they do is buy a house; then they purchase a life insurance policy, and thereafter a motorcycle. Motorcycles have been replacing bicycles for years. Usually, they are produced by Japanese manufacturers, or under license of a Japanese manufacturer, but increasingly now by Chinese businesses. The next step is the purchase of a car. At the beginning, it may be, for instance, a GM or a Volkswagen low-end vehicle. But the well-to-do people—or the people who have dramatically improved their living standards—go and buy European cars, such as Audis, Mercedes, Volkswagens, BMWs, and so forth; finally, they want dream cars, the likes of Ferraris and Lamborghinis.

Now I have to say that the United States is not really strong in these portions of the market. The same is true in fashion, cosmetics, or luxury. You have Ralph Lauren in the United States, but the Old Continent is much more dominant and has a lot to gain from the opening up of China and Eastern Europe and the increase of wealth that characterizes the newly industrialized world.

Sciarretta:	By the way, is it right that Chinese elites love expensive European wines?
Faber:	Yes, and there is a lesson to be learned here. In Asia, when affluent people entertain someone, they like to offer the best-quality products. Whether it is cognac or wine, they demand the best and most recognizable items so that their patrons know the goods are expensive. You want a Petrus wine on the table because it impresses your guest. The rich in Asia tend to exclude brands nobody knows and, therefore, in fashion, cosmetics, luxury, and high-end cars, Europe is a great beneficiary of the current state of affairs. I would recommend any company operating in those industries to work on the recognizability of their brands. That's

crucial to have success in Asia and gain a share of the upper-end customer.

Sciarretta: There's also a lot of hope about tourism: Sardinia, Saint Tropez, Venice, and southwestern Spain have already enjoyed waves of Russians spending lavishly in the bars, hotels, and shops. Now the continent looks forward to witnessing a pacific invasion of Asian people. If in the 1980s it was the Japanese with their Nikons, can we expect many more Chinese in the new millennium?

Faber: Although the Chinese and the Japanese are different from many points of view, there is a universal ambition and desire to travel. In time, I have no doubt that the Asians will represent the dominant group of travelers in Europe—the Chinese, Japanese, Koreans, and so on.

Sciarretta: Any investment idea you can connect with this trend?

Faber: I think of the airline industry. My thesis is simple: Airlines have suffered from a combination of weak demand, ferocious competition, and high oil prices. These unfavorable events have engendered bankruptcies, the disposing of weak divisions, cuts in corporate overhead, and, by and large, a concentration of market share. Whenever the economy recovers, the airline industry will move within a path of limited capacity: That is the time when profitability will come back.

Sciarretta: In the past you mentioned Lufthansa—Germany's flag carrier—as a company to keep on your radar screen.

Faber: Perhaps I would rather prefer, say, Singapore Airlines or Cathay Pacific in Asia, because they are directly exposed to the next boom in traveling and because, in my opinion, most Asian countries—including developed Japan, Australia, New Zealand, and South Korea—will over time become more Asia-centric, or, if you wish, more China-centric, while the role of the United States as a driving economic force will be diminishing. However, I also appreciate the merits of a company like Lufthansa, which is a powerful group in Europe and manages an important traffic with Eastern Europe.

Sciarretta: Dr. Faber, global investors must pay attention to currency movements: Would you talk a little bit about the dollar and the euro?

Faber: I am not enthusiastic about the euro, but I do think that the Eurozone is economically in a better shape than the United States and has politicians more inclined to oppose inflation. I imagine that as long as U.S. policymakers insist on a policy of printing and spending money as if there were no tomorrow, the dollar is doomed to remain in a long-run descending trend, even if it can experience sharp rallies now and then. I have said that Bernanke [the chairman of the Federal Reserve] is gold's best friend, and gold is the strongest currency around because its supply is more limited.

Sciarretta: A bullish story on the dollar could be as follows: Since U.S. households must whittle down their debt, consumer spending tapers off, saving rates go up, and imports from abroad go down. These changes result in an improving of America's external position and relieve the pressure on the dollar. What do you think about that?

Faber: The scenario you described is hardly convincing. The Federal Reserve follows a policy of targeting domestic consumption. If the United States does not consume, it means we are in a recession. Even more important, if the United States does not consume and the dollar is getting stronger, we are possibly in a deflationary recession. Under such circumstances, Mr. Bernanke would print money relentlessly and, in the process, undermine the position of the greenback.

Sciarretta: However, you do not seem particularly pessimistic about the outlook for U.S. stocks, do you?

Faber: In 2007, I believed equities were expensive and asked myself at what level I would buy again. I reasoned that if indexes were cut in half, I had to embrace a more optimistic stance. So, in March 2009 I turned bullish. After the bottom, the S&P 500 rebounded vigorously, but it is not as excessively priced as it was in 2007. Volatility, on the contrary, will stay high insofar as policymakers keep on flooding the markets with free money.

Sciarretta: Let's shift to Eastern Europe. You were early to predict a benign circle developing between Eastern Europe and core Europe in the 2003–2007 bull market. Then came the crash of 2008, and Eastern European banks, currencies, and stocks fell altogether. What's the outlook here?

Faber: Well, the first time I traveled to communist countries was in 1968, visiting Prague. At the time, people lived in miserable conditions and were constantly preoccupied with being thrown in jail by the state under whatever pretext. If you walk through formerly communist cities now, you are astonished to see how prosperous and advanced some of those societies have become in less than 40 years. For instance, you're Italian. If you happen to go on holiday in Slovenia [part of former Yugoslavia], you can appreciate a modern economy, not much different from Austria or Switzerland. A huge arbitrage has taken place that involves the price level, as well. In other words, it's no longer inexpensive traveling to Slovenia or buying property in the center of Prague.

Sciarretta: Would you say that the arbitrage process is over or that there's still something left to go for?

Faber: In general, of course, Eastern European wages are still lower than in Western Europe, and the populations want to catch up. This assures advantages for both parties. But, in my opinion, the big arbitrage opportunity created by a gigantic price and salary differential between Eastern and Western Europe has now gone.

Sciarretta: Do you see any out-of-consensus investment ideas in Europe?

Faber: Perhaps banks. They can beat consensus opinion, given the large involvement of the governments in their bailout. Further, the insurance industry can perform well, at least for a while, simply because it has the strength to constantly increase premiums.

Sciarretta: Do you have an investment opinion on Eurozone bonds relative to U.S. bonds?

Faber: They are okay now, but I have stayed more with corporate bonds in 2009, because the price was much more compelling; and I do not think that over the next 10 years bonds will do particularly well. In fact, inflation pressures are building up everywhere, and this does not speak in favor of bonds.

Sciarretta: If it comes to a choice between U.S. and Eurozone bonds, which would you choose?

Faber: I would choose Eurozone bonds for the reasons outlined above concerning currency risk and government attitudes toward inflation.

CHAPTER 12

Eastern Europe: The Prognosis Looks Favorable

AN INTERVIEW WITH MARK MOBIUS

Mark Mobius says that after Eastern European equity markets cratered in 2008, bargains abounded everywhere. In Russia you especially bet on commodities, of course. In the rest of Eastern Europe, you want to take a close look at consumer products because household incomes are on the way up. But you also want to consider manufactured goods, since production costs remain at a discount to Western Europe. And the storm of 2008? It decimated stock prices, so it's fully reflected in prices.

Mark Mobius has been a dominant figure in emerging-market investment for over 30 years. He is executive chairman of Templeton Asset Management and oversees $30 bn in emerging-market equities. Legend has it that even now, in his seventies, Mobius spends 200 days a year traveling between newly industrialized countries in search of investment opportunities. His style is bottom-up and value-oriented, based on company visits and close contact with the firms.

Vincenzo Sciarretta: Dr. Mobius, you have been investing in developing countries for some 40 years now. With this unparalleled background, how would you qualify emerging markets' valuations today: Would you say they are compelling, undervalued, fairly valued—or, on the contrary, expensive and risky?

Mark Mobius: Emerging markets were very cheap at the end of 2008. I did not envision stock prices going so low. Then came the fireworks and, generally speaking, the indexes shot up by over 70 percent. Since earnings prospects have brightened, I cannot say that stock prices have ceased being relevant to the fundamentals. The valuations are about in the middle of the 10-year high and low, so we can still find opportunities in bargain stocks, despite the rapid price rises.

Sciarretta: Are you indicating the emerging world is fairly valued?

Mobius: What I do claim is that, based on current estimates, market multiples—such as price-to-earnings, price-to-book, and dividend yields—look more or less in the middle of the historical range. Of course, it's a moving target and earnings estimates are subject to change, probably upward for a while. The encouraging part of the tale is that one can still discover lots of bargains out there. We continue to find companies selling at 10× price-to-earnings levels, price-to-book at 1.5× or less, and dividend yields of 4 percent or greater.

Sciarretta: Can you provide any anecdotal evidence of companies you regard as attractive in Eastern Europe?

Mobius: Recently I was in Russia visiting companies. We went to visit one of the largest hydroelectric plants in the country, owned by Rushydro, the listed hydroelectric company. I was very impressed by the facilities and how they were upgrading the control systems with equipment from Emerson of the United States. Rushydro's plants combined make it the second largest hydroelectric company in the world behind Hydro Quebec of Canada. However, the market capitalization vastly undervalues the company's assets. A few weeks after the visit, at one of Rushydro's plants there was an accident, and two large generators blew apart, causing millions of dollars of damage. We quickly looked at the impact on earnings and asset values and concluded that even with such a significant accident, the value of the company far exceeded its market value and its earnings capacity still had very great upside.

Sciarretta: I have read you're quite confident about Russia. Would you dwell on the bullish arguments?

Mobius: In the case of Russia, the commodity theme will predominate for some time, although there will be opportunities in the consumer area. A number of stocks fell dramatically, in many cases over 80 percent. Such extremes usually pave the way to investment bargains. It also seems that there is room to recover. Generally speaking, at Templeton we continue to find attractive opportunities in most sectors, despite the recent rally, as valuations remain low. A good example to illustrate the undervalued opportunities that are available in Russia is CTC Media, a Russian independent broadcasting company (controlled by Swedish MTG Broadcasting Group and the Altimo Group). In February 2009, the company listed on the NASDAQ with a market capitalization of $400 million, trading at a share price of $2.60. This was 82 percent below its June 2006 IPO price of $14, despite the fact that its earnings before interest, tax, depreciation, and amortization (EBITDA) had increased almost three times from 2005 to 2008. CTC media had a positive cash balance at the end of 2008, and it was not involved in any politics that could be viewed by foreign investors as a key business risk. The company was trading at an enterprise-value-to-EBITDA ratio of close to one, based on 2009 earnings estimations—a low price for a company in any industry but a very low price for a broadcasting company. However, CTC Media's share price has since rebounded and it is currently trading at $17 per share, or up 550 percent from its low in February 2009.

Sciarretta: The obvious objection is that shareholders have not always been treated fairly in Russia.

Mobius: The truth is that shareholders all around the world have not been treated fairly. Russia is no exception. From our experience, we have not been treated worse by Russian companies than by companies in other parts of the world, including the United States. In the EU, for example, the regulations forbid us to influence management, and in Luxembourg any holding above 5 percent is deemed to be influencing management. This kind of regulation clearly is bad for corporate governance, because as investors we should be doing our best to influence management to ensure that all minority shareholders are being treated fairly.

Sciarretta: That's a strong assertion, Dr. Mobius. Could you be more specific, please?

Mobius: What I am trying to point out here is that we are in a situation where every country has corporate governance problems. So we shouldn't really single out Russia. If you look at Enron, if you take the rating agency scandals, if you think about the banking crisis, well, I can't say that Russia is any worse. Of course, there are still instances where the violations of rules are obvious, but progress is being made, in our view.

Sciarretta: In the bull market of 2003–2007 a benign circle was set into motion where Eastern expansion proved to be disinflationary for core Europe and opened new markets for EU companies. At the same time, with lower wages and salaries, Eastern Europe attracted investment and production. Now, some argue that after the 2008 crash, the cycle has come to an end. Others disagree, reasoning that the crash was a test, and that after the test, the benign circle will reassert itself, with mutual benefits for Eastern and Western Europe. What do you think?

Mobius: No, the cycle has not come to an end, since countries in Eastern Europe are still quite competitive in labor costs and in some technical areas. The proximity to Western Europe means that Western European companies are still establishing manufacturing bases in Eastern Europe and acquiring Eastern European assets. More important, as per-capita incomes rise in Eastern Europe, those markets will become more significant consumer markets. The exciting thing about the European Union is that it is adding countries and expanding, so it is creating a larger market for goods and services, along with a legal structure that will enable companies to operate more easily within the entire region.

Sciarretta: How do you judge the health of the banking system in Eastern Europe after the 2008 crash?

Mobius: The banking system was hit badly, mainly because lots of their loans, particularly mortgage loans, were denominated in foreign currencies, such as the Swiss franc and the Japanese yen, in order to obtain lower interest rates. When some of the Eastern European currencies devalued against those currencies, the borrowers, and subsequently the banks, had problems. Of course, the degree of the problems is nowhere near the level of the subprime crisis in the United States, because of the embedded conservative mentality of Europeans generally.

Sciarretta: Again, this is a strong assertion. On the contrary, many commentators have emphasized that there was an affinity between the position of Eastern Europe in 2008 and that of the Asian Tigers in 1997. Would you turn to your personal experience for help?

Mobius: There's no question in my mind that Eastern European countries are not in the same condition as the Asia Tigers at the time. True, some banks made the mistake of offering mortgages in Swiss francs and Japanese yen. But Eastern European currencies did not fall as much as, say, the Thai baht, which lost 25 percent of its value in one day. And also the degree of leverage was nowhere near the level we saw in the United States with its subprime spree. Now, I am not saying it can't happen in the future, as banks become more sophisticated and an increasing number of people have bank accounts and credit cards, but we have not gone to that brink yet.

The other point about Eastern Europe is the presence of a big brother; I mean, Western Europe with Germany, France, and the EU authorities. They were willing to give support, provide confidence. What a mammoth difference from Asia, where the IMF came in and said, "Look, we can't really help; you have to tighten your belts." The IMF made things worse than they otherwise would have been. I do not neglect Eastern Europe's mistake of borrowing in foreign currencies, but the magnitude of the problems and their fallout look to me to be not as severe as they were in Asia.

Sciarretta: And when it comes to Russia?

Mobius: In Russia, the boom-burst sequence materialized when the oligarchs controlling large swaths of the economy took out gigantic foreign-currency loans to make overseas acquisitions. Domestic lending thus got into trouble as their oligarch clients experienced a liquidity crush, particularly when U.S. and West European acquisitions got into trouble.

Sciarretta: By and large, do you think Eastern Europe's mess is fully discounted by stock prices? After all, they plummeted like rocks.

Mobius: Yes, I believe that's the case. Since March 2009, we have been going through a recovery in stock prices, including Eastern banks and also Western banks with a large exposure to the east, such as the Austrian banks.

Sciarretta: What's the outlook for Eastern European currencies?

Mobius: In my opinion, the future is the euro. There will be an inexorable move to the single currency. The questionable requirements for joining the Eurozone imposed by the European Central Bank will probably fade away, making it easier for new countries to adopt the euro.

Sciarretta: What do you mean by "questionable requirements," and why are they questionable?

Mobius: For instance, I'm thinking of the 3 percent deficit-to-GDP ceiling, which is a cardinal rule to enter the euro. It is too rigid and does not consider other facts. We may miss the importance of bringing Eastern European countries within the Union. Let me give you an example: The vicissitudes of the Baltic States—namely Latvia, Lithuania, and Estonia—have been scary in 2008 and 2009, but if you look at the size of their reserves, they could adopt the euro tomorrow. It is my view that the benefits of putting other countries into the monetary union outweigh several possible hurdles. And, by the way, troubled Eastern markets and economies would recover much faster.

Sciarretta: Russia aside, are there any other Far Eastern countries particularly rife with opportunities?

Mobius: I would say—believe it or not—that Ukraine offers a good number of undervalued companies, despite the bad picture we receive from the press. My bullish thesis rests on the collapse of the currency. When currencies fall as much as has happened in Ukraine [where the exchange rate plunged by 40 to 50 percent in 2008–2009], the tradable sector is always relieved and opportunities arise.

Sciarretta: If in commodity-rich countries you act on the premise that natural resources show a strong trend, and given that raw-material stocks fell off the cliff in the course of the last bear market, what are the areas you like the most in the rest of Eastern Europe?

Mobius: I would bet on manufactured goods and consumer products. In manufacturing, Eastern Europe has a skilled and cheap labor force. Hungary, for instance, is currently a leading player in the pharmaceutical industry, and its exports are not limited to Western Europe and Russia. Rising per-capita income will gradually favor consumer-related industries. In the same group I put not only classical consumer goods and the media industry, but also consumer banks, that is, banks with exposure to consumers instead of corporations.[1]

Sciarretta: Vis-à-vis other emerging markets, how would you rate Eastern Europe in terms of how many attractive investments you find here and there?

Mobius: Eastern European countries fell markedly, and now opportunities abound everywhere. Of course, the problem for me is the size. If you look at our global portfolio, you see a lot of China up there, a lot of Brazil up there, because they are big, liquid markets. But Eastern Europe is fine. We stumble across bargains in all the countries of the region, without exception.

Sciarretta: What is the best asset for an investor who wants to ride Eastern Europe's recovery?

Mobius: Equities are at the top of our list. They have the best long-term upside.

CHAPTER 13

Europe Is Moving Toward the Center-Right, the United States Toward the Left

AN INTERVIEW WITH EDWARD YARDENI

D r. Edward Yardeni, president of Yardeni Research, is well-known as one of the best U.S. investment advisors and providers of independent global investment-strategy research. He previously served as chief investment strategist for Oak Associates, Prudential Equity Group, and Deutsche Bank. Moreover, he held positions at the Federal Reserve Board of Governors and the U.S. Treasury Department in Washington.

Vincenzo Sciarretta:	Dr. Yardeni, is the United States adopting a more social-democratic stance?
Ed Yardeni:	Social-welfare outlays continue to grow more rapidly than GDP, thus clearly the country is becoming more social-democratic in the sense that the government is providing more and more benefits to Americans. By the way, it is doing so by increasingly putting under strain our public finances rather than tightening up taxation.
Sciarretta:	Can you provide just one figure to summarize what you have just said?
Yardeni:	Yes. For instance, social benefits to Americans (as a percentage of compensation of employees) is moving toward 30 percent, while it was below 20 percent during most of the last three decades.

Sciarretta: What are the main areas where the United States is embracing a more social-democratic course?

Yardeni: Certainly in retirement and health-care benefits. The reality is that the U.S. government already pays for about 50 percent of health-care spending because of Medicare and Medicaid. No matter what sort of reform the Obama administration comes up with, the trend is that the government will be financing more and more of the health care of the United States.

Sciarretta: What about the fact that the state is standing head and shoulders above private industrialists in many sectors of the economy, such as finance, automobiles, or real estate? Do you think the incursion is temporary, or temporary until it becomes permanent?

Yardeni: We have seen the rising of industrial policy in the course of the financial crisis, but I do not think the authorities really want to be running the banking industry or the automobile industry or any other sector that can be managed better by private groups. Most of what we have seen during the financial crisis was on an emerging basis, and I do not believe that Washington is going to nationalize—either on a de facto or on a de jure basis—any major industry in the United States.

Sciarretta: After the Christian Democratic Union and the smaller Free Democratic Party won a surprisingly large majority in German parliament on September 27, 2009, you wrote that Europe was moving toward the center-right, while the United States was moving left. What did you mean?

Yardeni: Yes, Chancellor Angela Merkel immediately promised to lower income taxes, as well as reform corporate and inheritance taxes. The *Financial Times* observed that of the EU's six biggest states—Germany, UK, France, Italy, Spain, and Poland—four now have center-right governments, and Britain could join the club by next summer. (Spain has a center-left government.)

Sciarretta: Do you think the strength of the euro against the dollar may be connected in part with the political trends on the two sides of the Atlantic?

Yardeni: Currency markets do reflect not only present but also future economic conditions; also international capital transfers are notoriously influenced by political trends. And having more conservative governments running the economies of Europe may be more appealing to investors than the approach of the Obama administration.

Sciarretta: Any further implications?

Yardeni: It may very well be that European stocks outperform their U.S. cousins in local currency. If you're a U.S. investor and the euro is strong, then the move into European-listed companies may be attractive, because both stocks and the currency would work in your favor.

Sciarretta: Do you have a target for the euro against the dollar?

Yardeni: The single currency is likely to reach new records beyond the old peak of 1.60. I am a U.S.-based investor, so my focus is especially on the dollar and its weakness. The main concern right now is that our federal deficit is soaring. Of course, much of Europe has the same kind of problem, but the rate of change is much more significant in the United States in terms of debt variation and the move toward providing more social welfare.

Sciarretta: The euro is often treated as if it were the mirror image of the dollar. Yet, it has been strong against a large number of currencies such as the British pound and, by and large, the Asian currencies. In other words, it has its own merits. Can you cite any driving forces behind the rise of the euro that are not already widely recognized?

Yardeni: Yes, the euro has been surprisingly strong given that the Eurozone confronts many of the same problems in the financial system as we do in the United States. Part of the dynamism may be related to foreign investors' choices. Especially Middle East players seem to have a preference for the euro versus the dollar. They tend to travel more in the Old Continent and to invest more over there. I guess there is a political security issue to be considered as well. Some investors fear their capital might be frozen more easily in the United States than in Europe if things go wrong.

Sciarretta: Early in this interview, you argued that Eurozone stocks may react positively to the political movement of the continent toward the center-right. Do you believe that, by the same token, U.S. equities deserve a lower premium than in the past because the country is shifting toward more social-democratic, less free-market policies?

Yardeni: Not necessarily, because I see a way out: U.S. companies are decoupling from the U.S. economy, looking for growth overseas, eminently in the emerging economies. While I recognize that corporate America may have less exciting days at home, more and more companies are becoming multinationals, and more and more of the earnings growth will come from overseas.

Sciarretta: So if it comes to a choice between investing in Eurozone equities or investing in U.S. equities, the exchange rate becomes crucial, right?

Yardeni: Yes, that's right. I am inclined to believe that the dollar has more downside, in which case a strong euro may have an adverse impact on Eurozone exports and should give a boost to U.S. industrial companies.

Sciarretta: But that is in local currency.

Yardeni: Yes.

Sciarretta: And in common currency?

Yardeni: If you are a Eurozone-based investor, you will probably be better off staying at home.

Sciarretta: You were right to bet on technology, media, and telecommunications as the leading sectors of the 1990s; and then you were right again indicating materials, industrials, and energy as the outperformers of the 2003–2007 bull market. Where do you see the new leadership in the years ahead?

Yardeni: I think tech is back. Technology is one of the clearest ways to play the global expansion associated with emerging economies. As people prosper there, discretionary consumption ought to rise, and demand for TVs, mobile phones, and the like should jump. Semiconductors are among the main beneficiaries. This trend actually may help America against Europe, since technology is a bigger sector in the United States. It should be remembered that in 2003–2007 the S&P 500 lagged behind as technology's market multiples contracted dramatically, but in the late 1990s the opposite was true, because technology led the way up.

Sciarretta: Any other sectors?

Yardeni: I remain of the view that materials, industrials, and energy are likely to perform well in response to the demand emanating from the newly industrialized nations; however, if I had to pick one sector it would be technology, in the same way that during the bull market of 2003–2007 it was energy.

Sciarretta: Do you see any specific theme for the Eurozone?

Yardeni: Europe should pay a lot of attention to emerging economies because, with the euro going up, it is important to choose companies with a strong demand from those areas—demand that will not disappear if the single currency gains ground, such as in capital goods. Also, I would bet on health care, which will benefit from the aging population of Europe.

Sciarretta: The stock markets have had a sensational rebound from the March 2009 bottom. Now, in September 2009, how do you judge valuations?

Yardeni: I would say that stock indexes both in Europe and in America are fairly valued. The rally was fed by valuation-multiple expansion rather than earnings growth. From here onward, we need earnings to start to expand for the rally to be sustainable.

Sciarretta: And do you think that is likely?

Yardeni: Yes, I do.

Sciarretta: One can note that the stock markets tend to alternate between long-term bull advances and long-term sideways movements. For instance, from 1982 to 2000 or from 1942 to 1966 American stocks went up, while from 1966 to 1982 they zigzagged sideways. This time around, stocks in Europe and America topped out in 2000, and now ten years have passed, digesting the excesses of the 1990s. Do you expect we are in, or close to, a new secular bull market in Western counties?

Yardeni: Of course there is no way to know precisely. But when sentiment is so negative and pessimism so overwhelming, something usually comes out of nowhere and surprises on the upside. I am open to a positive scenario.

The surprise could be a political cycle less adverse to business than currently expected; it could be a revolution in the energy area; or the most obvious candidate: greater prosperity in emerging markets that lifts all of us alike. I tend to be optimistic. And even if the sideways movement is still in place, it is very wide, since stock indexes have been fluctuating between the 2000 and 2008 tops and the bottoms of 2003 and 2009. We are now in the middle of the range, and on the way up there is still good money to be made. In Europe and in the United States.

CHAPTER

14

For Now I Go with Continental Europe

AN INTERVIEW WITH KEN FISHER

Although very successful in the long run, Ken Fisher came up against a dramatic setback in 2008. I call a "dramatic setback" the simple occurrence that he did not anticipate the emergence of the bear market, and hence was severely penalized, along with most fellow managers. But that was the exception. Otherwise, Fisher has made some awfully timely calls on the bear side, predicting the Nasdaq debacle of 2000,[1] suggesting a retreat in September 1989, and pulling back in June 1987.

Who is Ken Fisher? The third and youngest son of renowned investor and author Philip A. Fisher, Ken is in his own right a well-respected investor and author. He has written six books. The first, *Super Stocks* (New York: McGraw-Hill, 1984), pioneered the use of price/sales ratios as a forecasting tool. The most recent, 2009 best-seller *How to Smell a Rat* (Hoboken, NJ: John Wiley & Sons), is about the "Five Signs of Financial Fraud." In addition to his several books, Fisher signs "Portfolio Strategy," a monthly column in *Forbes* magazine that he has written continuously for 25 years.

When we first conceived the idea of this book, Kenneth Fisher immediately came to my mind: He is a large and charismatic global investor who can move billions from one region to the next. Fisher is the founder, chairman, and CEO of Fisher Investments, a money-management company headquartered in Woodside, California. Fisher was counted by *Investor Advisor* magazine in the list of the 25 most influential people in and around the investment-advisory business, and *Forbes* magazine included him in the 2008 group of the 400 richest Americans. At the time of the interview (August 2009), his fund controlled $34 bn versus $44 bn before the bear market took its toll.

If the primary reason to call Mr. Fisher was his role as a major global manager, confronting every day the problem of how to allocate resources among the United States, the Old Continent, and the emerging markets, I must confess that I was also intrigued by his personal experiences during the brutal bear market of 2008. In speaking with him, I noted that Internet surfers were quite harsh when commenting on Fisher's bullish (and wrong) posture in 2008. They called him "arrogant," and that was one of the milder adjectives you could find. I was curious to know, how does a multibillion-dollar manager cope with the psychological pressure of being wrong and feeling like the target of bitter criticism? Could he sleep? What are his opinions about going right or wrong in the market? These were some of the questions that came to my mind, questions every investor, large or small, must look in the face. Accordingly, Fisher's interview is a little bit different from the others: In the first half, the discussion is about "what went wrong in 2008." In the second half the subject returns to the cardinal topic of the book: how to allocate between the United States and the Old Continent.

Part I: What Went Wrong in 2008?

Vincenzo Sciarretta:	Mr. Fisher, I have been reading your *Forbes* column for a long time, and 2008 was perhaps the first time you did not see a major stock market trend change arriving. What went wrong? What were your considerations?
Ken Fisher:	I failed to anticipate the negative and inconsistent actions of the Federal Reserve and U.S. Treasury under Secretary Henry Paulson: They went from problem company to problem company, managing them all very differently, confusing the forest for the trees and, in the process, frightening the lenders of overnight reserves upon which our system is based. This led to the credit markets freezing and locking up in mid-September. In my opinion, the Lehman bankruptcy has never been accurately depicted by the media in terms of what actually happened, and it was the linchpin. If our authori-

	ties had handled the situation better, I don't think we would have had September through March, nor the size of problems that came with them.
Sciarretta:	Personally, I have learned that every investor sometimes wins and sometimes loses, but I guess most clients would like to win all the time. I read on the Internet some surfers calling you "arrogant" for your market posture in 2008 and for not changing the route in due time. I imagine your nerves were sorely tested.
Fisher:	No, not really. I have been at this industry for 37 years and through good markets and bad. I've long described the market as The Great Humiliator, which exists for the sole purpose of humiliating as many people as possible for as long as possible for as much money as possible. It wants to get you, your readers, your mother—but even more it wants to get me. And my goal is to engage The Great Humiliator continually without ending up humiliated by it. I cover that in great length in my 2006 book, *The Only Three Questions That Count* [Hoboken, NJ: John Wiley & Sons]. In the same book I observe that the most legendary investors (present and past) are only right about 70 percent of the time, which means being wrong about 30 percent of the time. Yet those periods of being right and wrong often materialize in long, clumpy patches that can feel like they will continue forever and are, in fact, excellent fodder for The Great Humiliator.
Sciarretta:	What about the harsh comments that poured in on top of you?
Fisher:	Relative to what anonymous Internet surfers say about me, I don't pay attention. What they think isn't any of my business. There are today with the Internet always snarky people saying you're wrong, no matter what you're saying. In 2008 I was bullish and wrong. In 2009 I was bullish and right. In 2008 they said what you say they said. In 2009 they said either that I'm always bullish, which is false, or that this is a sucker rally in a secular bear market and that I'm an idiot. But The Great Humiliator—the market—doesn't really care at all what they think or what I think. It only cares about whether you're right or not. It isn't a popularity contest.

Sciarretta:	What is the mood of a big investor like you when markets bite and clients make you feel their weight? How can you preserve your balance? How can you sleep at night?
Fisher:	I don't relate to the question very well. I sleep easily at night in the worst of circumstances. It's just a matter of training yourself. It doesn't serve me or my clients or employees if I'm a wretch because things don't go well for a while. That would only make things go less well longer, because I'd be in a less-good condition to recognize things and get on track. It's kind of like a battlefield officer in the military. They have to train themselves to sleep when appropriate and necessary, while facing constantly adverse and hostile conditions.
Sciarretta:	What is your advice to a saver—or a client for that matter—who has to navigate through the ups and downs of the markets?
Fisher:	Always look forward, never backward, except to regard history as a laboratory-like learning experience. People tend too much to extrapolate the recent past into the future. The way people usually react to a bull market is to get more bullish, and to a bear market to get more bearish. It is better to get more bullish in the face of lower prices and less bullish in the face of higher prices. That's the rule. Unfortunately, that trapped me in 2008 because, as prices fell, I became more bullish, not seeing the dangers we have mentioned earlier. Still, being very bullish at the bottom was the right thing to do, and yet too many got less bullish. The other thing to remember is that bull markets run a lot longer than people expect. If you believe—as I do—that the bear market ended on March 9, 2009, then we are in the early stages of the new advance. Usually bull markets last three to six years, and hence there should be a lot still ahead.

Part II: Allocating Money

Sciarretta:	You are reported to benchmark against the MSCI World Index [consisting of stocks from all the developed markets in the world]. Is that true?

Fisher: We manage against a number of benchmarks, particularly on the institutional side of our business. But for most of our money, about 70 percent, yes, the MSCI World is our benchmark.

Sciarretta: In the old days, Fisher Investments was primarily a domestically oriented company, and more recently it has become a global player. What is the regional allocation of your funds around the globe?

Fisher: At present, we are slightly underweight to America, underweight to Japan, and heavily underweight to Britain. On the other hand, the portfolio overweights continental Europe and, even more so, emerging markets.

Sciarretta: Would you elaborate on your current preference for continental Europe versus the United States? Can you list three or four reasons?

Fisher: First, over history, we've had long cycles where the United States has led Europe, followed by the reverse. This oscillation is a natural cycle, and we are still in the period where Europe has been leading the United States; and while this will likely end in the next few years, it is still there now. In a sense this is a momentum argument.

Sciarretta: Then?

Fisher: Second, the bulk of the current problems, many caused by the government, originated in the United States. Third, Europe fell harder in the back half of the decline, and hence should initially lead during the market advance. Fourth, my hunch is that Europeans are more skeptical of America than Americans are skeptical of Europe. While the prevailing bias will change, it is as it is now.

Sciarretta: You did not mention that Europe is cheaper than America. Is that intentional?

Fisher: Definitely. Europe is cheaper, but cheapness is not predictive of where stocks go in the short or intermediate term. I know most people think otherwise, but we've done a lot of studies and there is no reality in history that being cheaper makes a region perform better soon. Moreover, cheapness is sometimes a function of sector composition. Partially, Europe is cheaper than America because it has higher weights in sectors that are less expensive, such as finance, materials, and industrials.

Sciarretta: Why are you pessimistic about the United Kingdom?

Fisher: One can apply all the arguments about the United States, and even a few more. Britain's stock market tends to perform most of the time someplace in between the continent of Europe and the United States. Further, today nobody likes Gordon Brown, and he can't be as expansive as America has been relatively to stimulus. Their other problems are very American-like.

Sciarretta: How do you choose equities and sectors worldwide?

Fisher: The one thing I want to emphasize is that when we look back over time, we can see a strong positive correlation among all the stock markets. So you have to think globally about which sectors you want to be invested in.

Sciarretta: And what is your selection process?

Fisher: In this phase my reasoning can be articulated as follows: When a category—not just a sector—has done better, as well, or not much worse than the broad market in the first half of a bear market, and then gets hammered much worse than average in the latter stages, that sector historically always goes on to do better than the mean in the first roughly third of the subsequent bull market. This is a little-known piece of the way markets work. I call it the depressed spring effect.

Sciarretta: Any real examples?

Fisher: This process leads me to materials, industrials, energy, and consumer discretionary. By the way, this bet is consistent with my stance that the economy may surprise on the upside. Perhaps not in absolute terms, but surely against the thick blanket of pessimism that buries it.

Sciarretta: Do you plan to keep these equities for a while, or not?

Fisher: My sense is that you want to hold them in the first half of the bull market—so, for a few years.

Sciarretta: What should we do with the banks? They were the core of the problem and are a large chunk of Europe's stock market.

Fisher: Banks led the way down—they didn't do better—so they don't fall into my preferred categories. There is a limpid similarity to what technology did in 2000–2003 or energy in 1980–1982. They strongly bounced from the bottom but then lagged for a number of years. At the beginning, financials recovered sharply from the chasm. People thought: Banks were killed on the way down, they'll go parabolic on the way up. That is transitory. It will not last. Banks will lag for years, as energy did in the 1980s or technology did in the 2000s.

Sciarretta: Trends don't last forever, and someday you will dismantle your overweight position in continental Europe to rebuild a vast exposure in the United States. Are you already thinking about that?

Fisher: Sure. It's not a decision I have to take right here or right now. Not immediately. But cycles of under- and over-performance tend to follow a wavelike pattern similar to the movement of money between growth and value stocks. Periodically one becomes attractive compared to the other, and money follows accordingly. But it does not last forever.

Sciarretta: How could events unfold?

Fisher: I would not be surprised if sometime in the next two years—maybe approaching the 2012 presidential election—we see a return of relative strength in U.S. stocks.

Sciarretta: And what causes the change?

Fisher: The seeds may be social and political. In the 1990s—after the reunification of Germany and the birth of the euro—investors looked at the Old Continent too pessimistically. That was the time when America was celebrating its technological boom, and this made people think of our nation as an undisputed economic leader. But most trends reversed with the bear market of 2000–2003. The general public began disliking George W. Bush more and more, especially the foreigners. The United States called for change and moved to the center-left with president Obama. Europe has not witnessed an equivalent call for change. In Germany, chancellor Angela Merkel, despite several problems, remains very popular. In Italy, although premier Silvio Berlusconi creates his own bunch of problems, he maintains large popular support. Again, I do not see a call for change. But the tide may turn in the future. In a couple of years, Europeans may get tired of their politicians. In the United States, as we get closer to the presidential election of 2012, Obama may veer toward the center of U.S. politics instead of just left of the center. The pessimism that has been building up about the United States may diminish, and U.S. stocks may reaccelerate. I repeat: That's not a decision I have to take right here and right now, but I would not be surprised if events unfolded as I have just said. More, I am prepared for them.

15

Looking for Gems in the Eurozone Bond Market

AN INTERVIEW WITH EMANUELE RAVANO

It is said that in the early Roman Empire, the rate of interest was similar across the whole territory.[1] Further, when in A.D. 33 there was a liquidity crisis and interest rates went up, loans were called in and land prices collapsed. The emperor Tiberius lent substantial sums to landowners. The deal was for three years and without interest; the hope was to restore liquidity.[2]

After almost two thousand years, the Continent again ventured into a single-interest, single-currency, single-monetary-policy structure that is called the Monetary Union. And its success has been sensational (until now). Already, in a speech in 2004,[3] European Central Bank president Jean-Claude Trichet noted that, "Gradually, from the end of 1997 . . . the future euro area market interest rates became aligned with the lowest market rates available, denominated in the most credible currencies."

An outcome of this historic development is the emergence of a large and credible bond market that is more and more actively traded by local and international players.

Okay, but where are the investment opportunities? For an answer I talked to Emanuele Ravano. He is co-head of PIMCO's European strategy team in London and specializes in the management of euro and sterling portfolios. PIMCO is nowadays credited as the best global bond player around, and its co-founder Bill Gross is semi-religiously referred to as The Bond King.

Vincenzo Sciarretta:	Mr. Ravano, how mature is the Eurozone bond market, just a decade from the inception of the single currency? Would you say it has exceeded or undershot expectations?
Emanuele Ravano:	To give an answer we have to look at both quantitative and qualitative factors.
Sciarretta:	Please go on.
Ravano:	For instance, quantitatively, we have to ask ourselves where the corporate market was 10 years ago. Well, in September 1999 there were just over 1,000 issues for a total amount of €373 bn. In September 2009 we have 1,711 issues for a corresponding €1,422 bn. So, certainly in terms of size, the Eurozone has grown up very effectively. In addition, we have a vivacious high-yield market and a vivacious leveraged-loan market. Corporate bonds are not as diversified as for the United States, but the amount outstanding is a success; you could not imagine a universe like this in any single member country. I also would claim that in the United States we used to have a greater number of market makers and hence greater liquidity, but with fewer players around, that has become a less differentiating factor.
Sciarretta:	And for government obligations?
Ravano:	The benefit of lower inflation and interest rates on the Continent is almost too obvious to be an engaging subject of discussion. Both of them converged on levels that are well below Germany's prevailing figures at the time when the euro was adopted. In other words, inflation and interest rates did not gravitate around an average of the old values that were recorded in Italy, France, Spain, and so on. They did not even gravitate toward Germany's figures: They did better. By far.
Sciarretta:	Where would you expect more?
Ravano:	I think it is a little bit disappointing that we have not seen more progress in the direction of forming a single government bond market where the Eurozone borrows as a supranational entity. We still live with as many government bond markets as the number of the European states, creating—by the way—problems for the acceptance of the euro as a reserve currency.
Sciarretta:	Is that a feasible project?

Ravano:	I don't know whether it is feasible or not. But the point is that the entire construction of the euro is visionary, and we should keep some of the visionary spark to go on. The risk is otherwise that we lose momentum and see things moving backward.
Sciarretta:	Who should spend the money borrowed at a supranational level?
Ravano:	My view is that Europe has institutions such as the Parliament or the Commission, but they don't have much power. Over time, the onset of a common bond market could go hand in hand with the enhancement of these institutions.
Sciarretta:	Could you mention any additional differences between U.S. and Eurozone bond markets?
Ravano:	I would rather note some specific features. To illustrate: The covered bond market, which serves as an important source of funding for the banks, is more developed in Europe than in the United States. In contrast, Europe does not have a big market for mortgage-backed securities or agency mortgage-backed securities—it happens that some European banks securitize a portion of their assets, but that's all.
Sciarretta:	What about corporate bonds?
Ravano:	The U.S. market is roughly double in terms of issues, with a total of about 3,880 versus 1,711 in the Old Continent. The dollar amounts, however, are about the same, with $2,719 bn in the United States and $2,076 in the Eurozone. So, I would say, diversification is better realized in America.
Sciarretta:	Let's move to the Eurozone's bond investment arena. Where are the opportunities?
Ravano:	I am especially thinking about three ideas:

1. Benefit from the shape of the yield curve.
2. Take a long position in euro investment-grade securities.
3. Get exposure to 30-year bunds, now yielding 4.1 percent.

Sciarretta:	Okay, let's start with point 1.
Ravano:	A convincing opportunity is linked to the present shape of the yield curve.[4] In recent months it has reached its steepest slope since the creation of the euro; namely,

the differential between 10-year yields and two-year yields is as high as it has ever been. The current difference is in fact over 2 percent, compared to an average level of 0.9 percent over the last 11 years [the conversation took place in August–September 2009].

Sciarretta: Why is that so?

Ravano: Historically, the slope of the curve has been a good leading indicator of economic activity, as it summarizes where investors believe interest rates are headed.[5] In my opinion, the steepness of the yield curve is clearly signaling a quick return to more normal growth following the 2008–2009 recession.

Sciarretta: That's the diagnosis; where is the opportunity?

Ravano: Fixed-income managers can seek extra return with a bond investment strategy known as riding the yield curve, or rolling down the yield curve.

Sciarretta: Can you explain it for a nonspecialist readership?

Ravano: Presuppose the yield curve slopes upward, which is the case in Europe today. As a bond approaches maturity or "rolls down the yield curve," it is valued at successively lower yields and higher prices. Using this strategy, a bond is held for a period of time as it appreciates in price and is sold before maturity in order to realize a gain.

Sciarretta: What about a concrete example?

Ravano: Say an investor buys a five-year German government bond at a yield of 2.4 percent and waits for a year. If you assume that yields remain unchanged, the bond will have become a four-year bond with a yield of 2 percent. This gives the investor a total return of 3.5 percent, equal to the yield he pockets, plus the appreciation of the bond (when the yield goes down, the price goes up).

Sciarretta: What's next?

Ravano: The investor can sell the four-year bond, realize the profit, and buy a new five-year bond at a higher yield. In practice, the yield curve does move, but the key principle is that a positive yield curve can be used to the investor's advantage. In current market circumstances— if interest rates are unchanged—a manager who buys a two-year German bund would gain almost 0.9 percent

	in addition to the yield via this "rolling-down" effect over one year. The total return to the investor under this scenario would be almost 2 percent, that is, double the return obtained on a one-year deposit.
Sciarretta:	You also mentioned, as investment idea number 2, that the purchase of corporate bonds represents an attractive bet.
Ravano:	Yes, I do think so. One of the consequences of the 2008 crisis is that corporate spreads have been and remain above the average of the last 10 years. The EMU Corporate Index (a Merrill Lynch index with average maturity of 4.8 years) yields 4.25 percent, showing a differential of 200 basis points over government rates. While this number is well below the height of 2008 (6.85 percent), it still exhibits a substantial and inviting differential versus government securities.
Sciarretta:	Why do you qualify it as "inviting"?
Ravano:	First, I observe that the annual losses on a single-A corporate portfolio over 30 years have been around 0.3 percent.
Sciarretta:	Is that percentage supposed to go up?
Ravano:	I guess so, because the last 10 years saw strong economic activity, while we now live in uncertain times. But even if the figure doubled, investors would be well rewarded for the extra risk. I add that the average yield spread between corporate and government bonds has been equal to 100 basis points for a similar A-rated corporate portfolio.
Sciarretta:	While it now hovers around 200 points, right?
Ravano:	Yes, and although I do not expect a quick return to below-average, the magnitude of the extra yield suggests that a "buy and hold" strategy still makes sense.
Sciarretta:	You bet on a decline of the interest-rate differential between corporate and government bonds. What might be a target?
Ravano:	The reduction may go further than currently envisioned. Probably below the average of the past 10 years—although not very quickly, as I have just explained. There is a noteworthy similarity between the outlook of Europe today and the position of Japan in

the 1990s: Since private debt was falling while public debt was mushrooming, the interest-rate differential reached very low levels. It can happen again.

Sciarretta: What are the most appealing corporate sectors?

Ravano: The market continues to offer a wide differentiation in spreads. Single-A industrials yield 170 basis points more than government bonds, while financials with a similar rating yield almost twice as much, at 330 basis points. The environment is clearly favorable to security selection.

Sciarretta: Do you like the financials group?

Ravano: Sure. In Europe there is a strong political will to support the "national champion" banks on the assumption that they are critical for domestic activity and in consequence will not be allowed to fail. Equity holders and subordinated bank holders might be penalized in the worst scenario, but it is difficult to see how the banks could sink like Lehman did in September 2008.

Sciarretta: Any other bet that could find an alley in government policies?

Ravano: Specialists may want to have a look at this: Buy three- to five-year covered bonds at a spread of 90 bps over swaps. The total return generated by "rolling down the curve" would be equal to 4.3 percent, assuming yields remain stable over 12 months.

Sciarretta: I hope most readers were able to follow that. Please go on.

Ravano: Yes, covered bonds are bonds issued by banks and backed by loans and other assets, so that their repayment is secured. The advantage is that the bonds have real collateral behind them and that collateral has very different dynamics than U.S. mortgages. The reasoning in favor of this trade is that you have a higher rating, AAA, a maturity of three to five years—which is the sweet spot for a "roll down the curve" strategy—and finally you have implicit support from the ECB's program of quantitative easing. The program supports the banks and allows them to securitize parts of their balance sheets, and this in turn ought to help a revival of lending activity.

Sciarretta: Now, what about an idea that could benefit a less sophisticated group of investors? As your third point, you mentioned German long-term government obligations.

Ravano: Yes, 30-year bunds yield a satisfactory 4.1 percent [real yield close to 5 percent]. My bullish bias hinges on the fact that deflationary forces are strong in the Eurozone, on account of demographic trends, undercapitalization of the banks, and limited fiscal response.

Sciarretta: What do you answer when the case is made that sooner or later the burden of accumulated debt will lead to inflation?

Ravano: I would answer that in the Eurozone the bet is asymmetric in favor of the holder of long-term bonds. If inflation accelerates, the ECB is mandated to neutralize the pressure. Remember, the European Central Bank has only one constitutional objective: containing inflation below, but close to, 2 percent.

Sciarretta: It seems to me that under the same policy, the ECB must also avoid deflation, since price increases should not fall much below 2 percent.

Ravano: Absolutely. Yet, I think the ECB is not perfectly equipped to confront the possibility of a deflationary spiral. To this end, it is essential that the central bank can employ an effective policy of quantitative easing. But here in Europe the main handicap is the absence of a single, unified government-bond market: If the central bank doesn't have a firm grip on bonds, it is more difficult to embark on a quantitative policy. Contrariwise, with one government bond market and one agency mortgage market, the U.S. Federal Reserve can engage in a campaign of quantitative easing more effectively. The conclusion is that if one wants to stay in Eurozone bonds, the place to be is the long end, because there an asymmetric opportunity does exist.

CHAPTER 16

The Path of Least Resistance Leads to a Stronger Euro and a Weaker Dollar

AN INTERVIEW WITH CATHERINE MANN

If one looks purely at the exchange-rate level that makes corporate America competitive in foreign trade versus corporate Europe, it could be argued that at 1.4 to 1.5 the dollar is reasonably valued against the euro. Yet, an additional fall in the dollar's value may be motivated by international capital flows, that is, market participants' preferences to allocate resources in one currency rather than another.

My interlocutor in this conversation is Catherine Mann, who has followed an enviable academic and professional path. She graduated from Harvard University and received her PhD in economics from the Massachusetts Institute of Technology. Mann has been senior fellow at the Peterson Institute for International Economics since 1997 and is a professor of economics at Brandeis University. She also served as assistant director of the International Finance Division of the Federal Reserve Board of Governors, on the President's Council of Economic Advisers at the White House, and as advisor to the chief economist of the World Bank.

Sometimes, it is things that are said as asides to the conversation that provoke our thinking the most, and listening to Mann, two such points caught my attention. First, U.S. investors historically have shown a strong home bias, that is, an elevated tendency to keep their investments at home. According to Mann, home bias for U.S.

citizens has been around 90 percent; that is, they have tended to keep about 90 percent of their wealth in dollars. The figure is much higher than for Europe, where home bias is historically about 70 percent. But the important thing is not the past composition of the pie, but rather the way it will change in the future. The interview with William Clark and our own research in Chapter 7 make us lean toward a scenario in which U.S. investors do allocate an increasing share of their wealth abroad because the purchasing power of the dollar is challenged. If this is the case, even a marginal shift in U.S. preferences may have a potent impact on the dollar, since Americans have such a very high home bias to start with.

The second point that caught my attention is that U.S. authorities may find it appropriate to keep monetary policy loose for a long period of time. Mann notes that if the dollar declines, the United States pays the interest to foreign lenders in a depreciating currency, and hence the burden of the real debt is more manageable (provided, of course, there is not a flight from U.S. Treasuries).

Vincenzo Sciarretta:	Investigating the prospects of the dollar/euro, one cannot help noting how much the euro has appreciated against the dollar since it bottomed out at around 0.84 in the autumn of 2000.
Catherine Mann:	The exchange rate is dictated by a variety of "fundamentals." In terms of foreign trade, the fundamentals are income and sourcing patterns. For capital flows, the fundamentals are risk, return, and diversification.
Sciarretta:	Let's start with the trade balance.
Mann:	As you mentioned, the greenback has halved its value versus the single currency, and this has favored an improvement in America's external competitiveness. On the trade side, at least vis-à-vis the single currency, the decline of the dollar is probably almost over. The depreciation has been and ought to be successful in favoring U.S. exports and in discouraging imports from abroad. At least vis-à-vis Europe.
Sciarretta:	And for the rest of the world?
Mann:	If we look at Asia in general, if we look at the Chinese currency in particular, but even if we look at the Japanese yen (at least until quite recently), the exchange rates have not adjusted enough. Against most of these

currencies the dollar is likely to fall by another 10 to 15 percent on account of trade balances and relative prices. It makes no sense that many of these countries have had great improvements in productivity and have sustained continual external surpluses, yet their currencies appreciate little against the dollar.

Sciarretta: What about capital flows?

Mann: The other big source of demand and supply in the market for currencies is represented by international capital movements. The question is: What do investors want to buy? For instance, the second half of 2008 witnessed a strong dollar rally, which was largely determined by a quick and decisive shift in market participants' bent: They fled into U.S. short-term government obligations.

Sciarretta: How should we think about capital transfers?

Mann: Well, investors have a portfolio of wealth: That's the pie. And they think about how to divide the pie among various currency and investment areas. The first choice regards the share they want to keep in their home country, and this is called the home bias. We know that national preferences may hinge on regulatory restrictions: In China the home bias for the average investor is almost 100 percent, not because they want to hold 100 percent of their investments in Chinese assets, but because limits on capital outflows restrict their options with regard to what they can buy from abroad.

Sciarretta: What are the figures in Western societies?

Mann: In many countries of the Eurozone, home bias is around 70 percent. In the United States it's closer to 90 percent, quite high. Since the introduction of the euro, these figures have come down a bit.

Sciarretta: If a German buys French stocks, do you consider it a domestic or a foreign purchase?

Mann: In this discussion, it is domestic, because the biggest issue about home bias is not the nationality, but the exchange-rate exposure, and German and French stocks are both in euros. I did some research when the euro was introduced, and it showed that, at the time, for an Italian, a French, or a German, it was cheaper to

	buy U.S. assets than to buy assets in another European economy. That's because the stock exchanges were less mature and so the transactions costs were high. But that's changed. The transactions costs have diminished and, with the euro, I now consider Europe a block.
Sciarretta:	You described the composition of the pie. What's next?
Mann:	We have to examine how investors allocate an additional hundred euros of wealth. Do they invest the additional euros using the same compositional decisions they have applied to their current portfolios or not? If they are going to diverge from the historical home bias, and invest the additional euros in some foreign investment, there could be potent repercussions in the currency market.
Sciarretta:	Is that happening now?
Mann:	We know what happened during the financial crisis of 2008. Foreign investors dumped all their risky assets and went into U.S. Treasuries. At the margin they said, "I am very risk-averse, I am going into an asset that I know is the most secure and liquid, namely U.S. Treasury securities, particularly short-term."
Sciarretta:	Will investors go back to their old investment patterns?
Mann:	As regards the dollar/euro, demand and supply for the currency are affected by two additional elements. One: The United States is going to be issuing much more debt because of the growing fiscal deficit. Two: If foreigners move further and further away from their old home bias in order to finance our fiscal deficit, they presumably will ask for higher and higher interest rates. They may be willing to fund the United States, but at a higher return. Moreover, if they suspect that the dollar is going to depreciate, they will want to be compensated.
Sciarretta:	What is the most realistic outlet?
Mann:	The relationship between higher interest rates on U.S. debt and the dollar constitutes a fascinating issue. Higher interest rates make it more expensive to finance the U.S. debt. On the contrary, a lower dollar actually makes the value of the debt depreciate to the foreign

holder. So, I am guessing that policymakers will not offer too high a yield, because it would render our debt more expensive in real terms. The consequence is that the financial side of the equation pushes for a lower dollar.

Sciarretta: But if in 2010 the U.S. economy picks up somewhat, what are the odds that the Federal Reserve raises the cost of money significantly?

Mann: Pretty low, in my opinion. I don't see the Fed becoming very restrictive any time in the next three years. The labor market is expected to remain soft. And this is a central bank that believes inflation expectations are anchored and that globalization will effectively keep at bay any price increases emanating from a tight market for goods and services. In short, the Federal Reserve believes there's a lot of room to keep monetary policy expansionary for a prolonged period of time.

Sciarretta: In researching this book, I have noted that several U.S. managers are taking into consideration an enlargement of their exposure abroad to hedge the risks of a weak dollar.

Mann: U.S. investors, because home bias is so high, have a lot of room to buy foreign assets. We have a lot of wealth, still, and small changes in our preferred asset allocation toward foreign markets would exert a negative impact on the dollar. That is a trend to watch carefully.

Sciarretta: There is a wide discussion on whether loose monetary policy coupled with unprecedented fiscal deficits may lead to raging inflation in the United States. Do you have an opinion?

Mann: Yes, I have an opinion, and my opinion is that inflation is only a specter that will not materialize. Let's think about the theory of where price pressures come from. A first possibility is money growth, and we have that. The second source is changes in inflation expectations. This is a point that remains unresolved at present— some say that increases in gold and in TIPs point to rising inflation expectations. But the third source of price pressure that can feed inflation surfaces when tight economic conditions—both in the labor and product markets—enable prices to go up. On this crucial topic, I think we are a long way away from a danger zone. Capacity is abundant—for both product and labor markets. And even if capacity gets tight in one country, globalization keeps price dynamics under control.

So, if I ponder the three forces at work, I believe that inflation is a good story—certainly, it has theoretical foundations—but it is not a story that is going to play out for the next three to five years.

Sciarretta: Let me go back to America's external position: In 2008–2009 the trade deficit diminished to some degree. This amelioration is structural if it is associated with a lasting improvement in trade competitiveness. Vice versa, the adjustment is temporary if better trade figures merely reflect lower imports, due to the abrupt recession of 2008–2009. In the latter case, as soon as demand in the United States breaks out of its doldrums, imports boom, and the trade deficit returns to the starting point. Now comes the question: Choosing between the two diagnoses, how much of the trade deficit narrowing is structural and how much is temporary?

Mann: We have to think about the evolution of the trade deficit in response to changes in final demand (the recession) and in response to changes in relative prices (the exchange rate). As far as the demand is concerned, the improvement so far is mostly likely to be transitory. The sharp drop in U.S. GDP precipitated an equally resounding drop in U.S. imports that outweighed the fall in exports.[1] When the U.S. economy recovers, demand comes back to life, and the import-export balance worsens again.

Sciarretta: And what about the structural correction of the deficit?

Mann: That is due to a falling dollar. The bulk of the trade adjustment has happened against Europe and Latin America, much less against Asia, where the currencies have not moved as much as the euro versus the greenback. The main driver of the adjustment between Asia and the United States rested on a temporary fall in demand from the U.S. consumer. This is not structural;

this is transitory. I am convinced that the Chinese poli-cymakers will be reluctant to allow their exchange rate to go up. At some point, I suspect even the European authorities will be concerned about how to arrest the uptrend in their money.

Sciarretta: Do you have a target for the dollar/euro?

Mann: In 2008, the euro topped out around 1.60. Remember, before the financial crisis the level of worldwide activity was ebullient. There was plenty of demand for Eurozone exports. Despite a road-roller currency, EMU producers were able to compete effectively because global demand was strong. If the euro flexes its muscles again in 2010, that ought to occur against a scenario of much weaker international activity: Exporters would run into trouble because a lot of demand has vaporized. In sum, I would be surprised if in 2010 the euro had to break on the upside beyond the old peak of 1.60.

Sciarretta: I'll tell you what I have in mind: No nation has ever got richer by systematically devaluing its currency.

Mann: True. But an appreciating euro will bring windfall losses to exporters and may encourage a reallocation of man-ufacturing abroad—that is not a pleasant outlet when global growth is unsatisfactory. In addition, the holders of dollar-denominated assets lose wealth.

Sciarretta: In our interview, you have outlined a scenario, poten-tially lasting for years, where the United States cohabits with high deficits, loose monetary policy, and a weak trade balance—those do not seem handbook condi-tions for a strong currency.

Mann: No, they are not. Unless, of course—for some reason—we observe an influx of money into U.S. assets. It hap-pened in 2008. Or, if the rest of the world is slower to get out of recession than America is, the dollar may react positively, because capital owners would have an inducement to look at the United States for their investments.

Sciarretta: As we speak, gold is setting records beyond the $1,000/ounce threshold. Some commentators are raising the question whether such behavior may be symptomatic of an upcoming dollar crisis. Your opinion?

Mann: Gold gains are a sign of vast amounts of liquidity in search for a place to go.

Sciarretta: Not of a dollar crisis?

Mann: No. I do not see a one-way opportunity to sell the dollar short. Further, it wouldn't be in anybody's interests—foreign exporters lose markets, and holders of U.S. debt lose purchasing-power value of their wealth.

Eurozone Stocks: When Optimism Prevails

AN INTERVIEW WITH FRANÇOIS-XAVIER CHEVALLIER

W ould you like to know something?" said François-Xavier Chevallier in one of our phone conversations. "Debt is not as excessive as most point out. Leverage is huge in America, but the planet is larger than America. If you divide worldwide debt by worldwide equity, you don't get such an alarming figure. The background ought to be positive for stocks."

Chevallier lives in Paris, is married, and has two children. He got an MBA in 1973 from the University of Chicago, where his illustrious mentors included Arthur Laffer, Milton Friedman, Fisher Black, Eugene Fama, Merton Miller, and Gary Becker. In 1973, Chevallier began his financial career as international equity portfolio manager with Caisse des Dépots Paris and, later on, he joined BNP in the same position. After the merger with Paribas in 1999, Monsieur Chevallier became head of strategy and research. In 2001, he moved to CM-CIC's brokerage arm as chief strategist.

Founder and president of Alpha Mining SAS, a Paris-based investment consulting firm, he uses an ETF, sector-rotation proprietary model, on the argument that sector discrimination can be a major source of outperformance in the equity markets.[1] Chevallier is also the author of two books: *Le Bonheur économique* (Paris: Albin Michel, 1998) and *Greenspan's Taming of the Wave* (London: Kogan Page, 1999).

Vincenzo Sciarretta:	So, you expect positive economic activity and good stock returns for the next few years. What's the picture?
François-Xavier Chevallier:	Yes, I am leaning toward a scenario of reasonable GDP growth, low inflation, and correcting debt levels. By and large, it is a fertile ground for stocks—at least until inflation kicks in, probably a few years down the road.
Sciarretta:	Let's discuss why debt is not out of control.
Chevallier:	I use a gearing ratio calculated this way: First, I take all bonds listed worldwide, both private and public. Then I pass to all equity markets. Finally, I divide worldwide debt by worldwide equity and get the result. This is WorldBondMarketCap to WorldEquityMarketCap.
Sciarretta:	What is the story?
Chevallier:	In 1990 the ratio topped out at 2, because bonds were worth $16 trn and equity markets $8 trn. That was when Japan was leveraged to the hilt. After that, indebtedness to equity markets began to decline. In 2007, just before the subprime mess, the ratio was 1.2: Bonds were worth $80 trn, equities $65 trn. When I argue that the world was not especially leveraged, I am calculating an average. The United States was unbelievably leveraged, but planet Earth not so much.
Sciarretta:	Europe?
Chevallier:	In Europe, you have to separate Germany from the rest of the Continent. Germany was more a lender, the rest of the continent a borrower; on the whole, Europe was not an inveterate debtor.
Sciarretta:	And developing countries?
Chevallier:	On average—I stress, on average—their gearing ratio was low because equity markets had taken off while, at the same time, debt levels were more moderate. If you put it all together—United States, Europe, and emerging economies—the debt-to-equity ratio was not horrible in 2007. I repeat, America was more leveraged than at any time since the Great Depression, but the world as a

whole was not, because the virtues of the newcomers compensated for the vices of the United States and, to a lesser extent, of Europe.

Sciarretta: But with the 2008 crash everything changed, right?

Chevallier: Yes. Global equity markets were cut in half, and that was the denominator of the ratio. By contrast, only corporate bonds suffered a deep setback, while government bonds gained ground or were relatively stable. Therefore, worldwide debt-to-equity instantly shot up and reached levels similar to when Japan was sitting on a gigantic bubble. It is a strange pattern, I am aware, but with the rebound of stocks and other assets, it seems to me that the debt-to-equity ratio is correcting on its own accord and is moving toward values that are more or less acceptable, although the regional situation is rather diverse.

Sciarretta: That's good news. It implies no deflation or stagnation is ahead of us.

Chevallier: Exactly. I use two arguments in arriving at this conclusion. The first is that the theory of debt deflation, with its crashes and depressions, is well known to central banks, and they are doing whatever is necessary to avoid such an inauspicious outcome. The second point is that we are in a phase of the economic cycle where the emergence of the newly industrialized nations is such a major source of strength that a depression looks very unlikely.

Sciarretta: For a nonspecialist readership, would you explain what "debt deflation" means?

Chevallier: In a seminal article written in 1933, economist Irvin Fisher described the causes of the Great Depression as a chain of events: "It all starts from an asset bubble bursting out. Distress sales by individuals allow a partial repayment only of their bank indebtedness, which is followed by a decrease in bank deposits, an element of the money supply. A decrease results in a fall of the price level. Banks must also write off losses and their capital base shrinks, causing a decline in their net worth and hence bankruptcies. In turn, as the credit machine stalls, production sales and employment will then decrease, thus destroying confidence a little more, once again slowing the circulation of a reduced money supply. Nominal rates go down but real rates remain high."[2]

As you see, Fisher was the first economist to describe what a systemic crisis is all about, stressing that monetary disturbances (inflation or deflation) and overindebtedness are the two evils that really threaten growth. Now, since the years of the Great Depression were so vivid and dreadful, governments and central banks are opposing the forces of deflation with all their means. And I believe they are winning. My optimism is reinforced by the fact that we are not in a phase of the long-term cycle where a depression is expected.

Sciarretta: In what part of the cycle are we?

Chevallier: I use Kondratieff waves as a framework to analyze the future course of events.[3] In brief, economic history repeats itself every 50 to 60 years, with long phases of expansion followed by phases of downturn of equal duration. I think a new upturn occurred roughly in 1997 when the BRICs (Brazil, Russia, India, China) entered the free market. The trend is gaining traction, not losing it. Suffice it to say that, lately, the G-20 has been supplanting the G-7. Since upwaves of prosperity may last 20 to 30 years, we are not even halfway along that road. Stock markets still have some upside before inflation kicks in and really hurts.

Sciarretta: How do you see the Eurozone economy in the next few years?

Chevallier: Before 2008, we had strong economic activity and no inflation. Now, economic activity will be lower, but still satisfactory. Inflationary pressures are building up, since commodities are rising and monetary policy is expansionary. Instead of bursting out soon, inflation will bite in three to five years, because now there is too much excess capacity around. Leverage is a serious but manageable problem. All in all, the climate is good for stocks.

Sciarretta: Which ones do you like?

Chevallier: I am not a stock picker; I go with sectors.

Sciarretta:	For instance?
Chevallier:	A theme I like regards the aging of our population. The continent is really getting older. Now I shall name some companies; but they are not recommendations, they are just examples a reader can start from in developing his or her own research. In connection with aging, I cite Orpea [France], which works in the field of retirement homes, rehabilitation clinics, and psychiatric care. And Audika, which is a French company that offers hearing correction consultancy and solutions for hearing-impaired people. In health care, two illustrations can be Fresenius in Germany and Bio-Mérieux, exchanged on the Euronext.
Sciarretta:	What else?
Chevallier:	The new Malthusian constraints imposed by the scarcity of resources (food, basic materials, agricultural land, water, energy) and the forthcoming climatic changes are offering a lot of opportunities for investors. Again, just as examples to start from, one may want to look at utilities involved in water and waste management, such as Veolia [France] and Suez Environment [France].
Sciarretta:	If you believe in the green economy, you believe in renewable energy.
Chevallier:	Yes. I am an ETF investor, so I tend to reason in terms of homogeneous groups, and I think that renewable energies are attractive. Here are some names that exemplify the trend: EDP Renovaveis in Portugal and EDF Energies Nouvelles in France. In the windpower industry, you have Gamesa in Spain, Nordex in Germany, or Vestas Wind Systems in Denmark. In the photovoltaic area, some firms that come to my mind are Conergy, Solar World, Solar Millennium, and Q-Cells in Germany. Finally, I name Schmack Biogas, a Germany-based service provider in the biogas sector.
Sciarretta:	Do you expect a revival of the nuclear industry?
Chevallier:	Yes, I do. France generates some 78 percent of its electricity from this source. Global demand should be on the rise. Areva and EDF are two French companies that may benefit.

Sciarretta: Any other theme related to the green economy?

Chevallier: Yes, electric cars may have a future. You look at businesses that focus on specialty mechanical engineering, such as the German GEA Group, or at automakers such as Renault or Peugeot. But remember that they are just examples. You may also consider the sector of transport equipment and technology, with names such as Alstom, Schneider, and Siemens. Finally, in a green economy, chemicals ought to expand their business.

Sciarretta: Examples?

Chevallier: Air Liquide, exchanged on the Euronext, is a supplier of gases to a variety of industries such as food, automobiles, metal manufacturing, electronics, and pharmaceuticals. In Germany, I would look at Wacker Chemie; then I would analyze Linde, which operates in the gases and engineering sector, and KS [formerly Kali und Salz], which is an agricultural chemical and salt firm. Again, I am citing these stocks as a group, not as specific recommendations.

CHAPTER

18

The Credit Crunch Fallout Is Dreadful Everywhere (but the Eurozone Can Survive)

AN INTERVIEW WITH BOB MCKEE

I considered an interview with Bob McKee essential for this book, as he was one of the few analysts to prognosticate not only the ruin of the subprime market, but also the terrible shockwave that would radiate from it. When, in the autumn of 2007, he and his colleagues at Independent Strategy announced that the crisis could generate losses of $1.3 trn, people laughed in their faces.[1] Yet—once again—Cassandra was right. Or to be more precise: Reality exceeded worst expectations and financial markets had to be rescued by government interventions.

McKee joined Independent Strategy in 1994 as international economist. The firm, owned by David Roche and his partners, is headquartered in London and has gained a reputation for conceiving unbiased, prescient assessments of investment opportunities.

I was eager to interview McKee, and for a good, simple reason: In the Eurozone, the share of banks and financials is much larger than in the United States. Finance is 26.4 percent of the DJ EURO STOXX benchmark, while just 13.7 percent of the S&P 500 Index. And when it comes to banks, the sector accounts for 15.2 percent of market capitalization in the Eurozone, but just 3.9 percent in the

Table 18.1   Finance and Major Banks Weights as of July 2009

Country	Index	Finance	Major Bank
Eurozone	DJ EURO STOXX Bench	26.4%	15.2%
U.S.A.	S&P 500 Bench (US)	13.7%	3.9%
Germany	DAX Price Bench (DE)	21.7%	7.6%
France	CAC 40 Bench (FR)	19.2%	12.1%
Italy	FTSE/MIB Bench (IT)	45.2%	27.5%
Spain	Ibex 35 Bench (ES)	40.2%	37.2%

Source: FactSet

United States. (See Table 18.1, which shows finance and major bank weights as of July 2009.)

Thus a detailed, objective, and qualified discussion of the health of the financial sector was crucial to this project. If European banks were on shakier ground than their U.S. counterparts, it would have been difficult to speak of Eurozone outperformance. But that is not the case: Eurozone financials are in better shape than you might think (at least in relative terms). Here are McKee's thoughts and data.

Vincenzo Sciarretta:	In Europe and in America, banks have been recovering faster than many expected. What do you think about that?
Bob McKee:	The role of monetary authorities has been of paramount importance in sparking off the rally for both banks and the equity markets. Think of the Federal Reserve: It now owns 3 percent of the outstanding stock of U.S. Treasuries and 12 percent of agency mortgage debt. In sum, it exceeds $1 trillion.
Sciarretta:	That is good money for bad money.
McKee:	Yes, financial institutions that previously were stifling under the weight of these dubious assets now have good old cash. They don't want to hold much of it, since it earns little. And they have been reallocating something on the order of $400 to $600 bn to equities and additional liquidity to other financial commitments. It is easy for the banks to make profits in the current setting of free money. The moment of truth will come when interest rates start to normalize.

Sciarretta:	I would like to take an X-ray of the banking system on the two sides of the Atlantic and establish their relative health conditions. Just to start: What is the total amount of losses caused by the financial tsunami of 2008–2009?
McKee:	The IMF puts the total loss to the global financial system from the credit crunch at $3.4 trn.[2] We are less pessimistic and come up with an estimate of about $3 trn (after recoveries from defaulting assets). The banks alone will take a hit of over $2 trn. Separating by region, our best forecast is United States, $976 bn; Eurozone, $750 bn; UK, $240 bn; rest of the world $70 bn. I want to emphasize, however, that total bank assets in Europe are three times larger than those of U.S. banks, so the percentage hit to assets is much less in Europe.
Sciarretta:	You are speaking of the final amount of losses that is currently predicted, but what is the quantity already recognized?
McKee:	According to the latest data,[3] global admitted losses for all sectors of the financial world have touched $1.6 trn. Regionally, they have fallen on the United States at $1.1 trn, the Eurozone at $350 bn, the UK at $150 bn, and Asia at just $40 bn.
Sciarretta:	By "admitted" do you mean losses already reflected in the balance sheet?
McKee:	Yes, I do.
Sciarretta:	And what are the admitted losses for the banking sector alone?
McKee:	The number is $1.1 trn, of which $600 bn is the United States, $340 bn the Eurozone, $120 bn the UK, and $40 bn Asia.
Sciarretta:	Well, now I need to summarize the figures in order to understand better: You are saying that the U.S. banks have already suffered about 60 percent of their ultimate losses ($600 bn of $976 bn), while Eurozone institutions have admitted about 45 percent ($340 bn of $750 bn). Is that right?
McKee:	Yes, exactly. The European Central Bank [ECB] says Eurozone banks face another $300 bn in losses. We reckon $400 to 500 bn. From these estimates you can get an order of magnitude.

Sciarretta: The key question now is whether the banks and the other financial players (insurance companies, pension funds, and hedge funds) have raised enough capital to cover future losses, assuming that these institutions can also make profits from here on to restock capital reserves. What's your answer?

McKee: The latest data[4] show that, globally, financial institutions have raised $1.3 trn in new capital, both from state and private investors. This compares to estimated losses of $1.6 trn.

Sciarretta: And regionally?

McKee: U.S. institutions have raised $750 bn against losses of $1.1 trn; European institutions have raised $460 bn to nearly match losses of $500 bn.

Sciarretta: For the banks alone?

McKee: They have raised $1.1 trn in new capital to cover losses of $1.2 trn. The U.S. banks got $500 bn to cover $600 bn in losses, and European banks raised $450 bn to cover $460 bn.

Sciarretta: That doesn't seem so bad.

McKee: Yes, but remember that half of this capital raising has come from the taxpayer. However, the crucial question concerns the future. Based on our estimate of future writedowns and losses through to end-2010, we reckon that banks globally need to raise another $200 bn to achieve the barest minimum capital-adequacy ratio and achieve normal credit growth through to end-2010. To restore pre-crisis levels of tier-one capital under Basel-II, the banks need to obtain another $365 bn; and to achieve the higher adequacy levels now envisaged by the United States and UK at recent G-20 meetings, they would need $1.1 trn. All in all I would say the United States needs $250 to 400 bn and Europe $100 to 350 bn, depending on the regulatory requirements.

Sciarretta: Considering that trillions seem like peanuts nowadays, who cares about a few additional hundreds of billions?

McKee: Well, unless governments are prepared to come in with another bailout, banks globally will be unable to expand credit for some time ahead as they try to raise reserves

	and capital to meet adequacy levels. This is the inevitable hit to future economic growth.
Sciarretta:	But if asset prices go up and credit markets improve, wouldn't the need to attract new capital become less imperative?
McKee:	Yes and no. That would render marking to market less disastrous for writedowns on the balance sheet; but if borrowers default on debt—mortgages, credit cards, business loans, and corporate debt—then the losses cannot be escaped. I would also underline that future credit trends will be influenced by future regulatory choices.
Sciarretta:	What do you mean?
McKee:	Eurozone banks have higher leverage if it is measured by total assets to pure equity capital. But when measured using Basel-II for tier-one capital (namely, risk-weighted assets versus equity, plus reserves. etc.), and the same accounting rules for value are applied as in the United States, then there is little difference between U.S. and European banks. The G-20 appears to propose a cap on leverage at 25 times, and that is based on assets to tangible equity. It would be disadvantageous to Eurozone banks. On the contrary, if Basel-II is maintained, it would be less negative for the Old Continent.
Sciarretta:	Can the banks help an economic recovery?
McKee:	My short answer is that the banks will not help for the next two years at least unless they can raise more capital and that implies more state funding of perhaps $200 to $500 bn. In my opinion, this is an unlikely outcome. So assuming no large bank goes bust, the most realistic scenario is the Japanese syndrome: Banks don't lend much and instead use profits to build up capital reserves/provisions to deal with future losses.
Sciarretta:	The financial crisis has been accompanied by a huge cost to the taxpayer. Can we provide any numbers?
McKee:	According to the ECB, Eurozone governments have committed a total €795 bn ($1.1 trn) in bailout packages, with about €200bn of that in capital injections or asset purchases. In Table 18.2 you can see the EU

Table 18.2 Euro-Area Public Interventions in the Banking Sector (in % of GDP, Jun. 2008 to Apr. 2009)

	Capital Injections		Guarantees on Bank Liabilities		Relief of Impaired Assets		Liquidity and Bank Funding Support		Total	
	Approved	Effective	Approved	Effective	Approved	Effective	Approved	Effective	Approved	Effective
Austria	5.0	1.7	25.7	5.1	0.4	0.4	1.6	1.5	32.8	8.7
Belgium	4.2	5.7	70.8	16.3	4.2	4.2	na	nr	79.2	26.2
Cyprus	0.0	0.0	0.0	0.0	0.0	0.0	0.0	0.0	0.0	0.0
Germany	4.2	1.6	18.6	7.1	0.4	0.4	0.0	0.0	23.2	9.1
Greece	2.0	1.5	6.1	1.2	0.0	0.0	3.3	1.8	11.4	4.6
Spain	0.0	0.0	9.3	3.2	0.0	0.0	2.8	1.8	12.1	5.0
Finland	0.0	0.0	27.7	0.0	0.0	0.0	0.0	0.0	27.7	0.0
France	1.2	0.8	16.6	4.5	0.2	0.2	0.0	0.0	18.1	5.6
Ireland	5.1	4.2	225.2	225.2	0.0	0.0	0.0	0.0	230.3	229.4
Italy	1.3	0.0	na	0.0	0.0	0.0	0.0	0.0	1.3	0.0
Luxembourg	6.9	7.9	12.4	nr	0.0	0.0	0.0	0.0	19.3	7.9
Malta	0.0	0.0	0.0	0.0	0.0	0.0	0.0	0.0	0.0	0.0
Netherlands	13.9	13.9	34.3	7.7	3.9	3.9	0.0	7.5	52.2	33.1
Portugal	2.4	0.0	10.0	3.3	0.0	0.0	0.0	0.0	12.5	3.3
Slovenia	0.0	0.4	32.8	0.0	0.0	0.0	0.0	0.0	32.8	0.4
Slovakia	0.0	0.0	0.0	0.0	0.0	0.0	0.0	0.0	0.0	0.0
Euro area	3.0	1.9	20.5	8.7	0.6	0.6	0.5	0.8	24.6	12.0
Memo EU-27	2.9	1.8	24.6	8.1	0.4	0.4	2.5	2.6	30.5	13.0

Notes: na—Not available indicates that the amount is not available in the State aid decision.

nr—Not reported indicates that the amount was not reported by the Member State in its reply to the EFC questionnaire.

Source: Commission services.

Commission's estimate of state support for the banking sector.

As regards capital injections and asset purchases alone, it adds up to 3.6 percent of GDP approved and 2.5 percent of GDP spent for the euro area: It is much less than in the United States or the UK.

Sciarretta: What are comparable figures for the Anglo-Saxons?

McKee: According to the IMF's public finances report, March 2009, the comparable figures for the United States would be 10 percent of GDP, with 6.3 percent spent; and for the UK 17.3 percent of GDP, all of it spent. Of course, there will be paybacks and recoveries, but I expect a net loss to the taxpayer approaching 6 to 8 percent of GDP before we are done. For the United States we have attempted our own calculations, and the impact is striking: This "credit crisis" has cost 12.7 percent of GDP, excluding liquidity support. In perspective, the cost is 10 times as high as the savings and loan crisis and more than twice the Vietnam war. (See Table 18.3.)

Sciarretta: What should investors do with bank stocks? Should we buy, hold, or sell?

McKee: U.S. and European banks have become very cheap historically, and their stock prices have actually outperformed the market since the crisis began!

Sciarretta: Really?

Table 18.3   Financial Crisis: A Terrible Cost to the U.S. Taxpayer

	Historical Cost*	Today's $	% of GDP
WWII	288	3600	25.7
Credit crisis	**1775**	**1775**	**12.7**
War on Terror	1000	1100	8.0
Vietnam War	111	698	5.0
New Deal	32	500	3.7
S&L crisis	153	256	1.8
Marshall Plan	12.7	115	0.8

*Billion dollars
Source: Independent Strategy

McKee: Yes, check the performance of the banking sector against global equities since July 2008 and you'll see I'm right.

Sciarretta: Is the rebound justified?

McKee: In my opinion, investors are far too optimistic about the banks. Banks have turned around because of government capital and loan guarantees, plus a huge influx of liquidity at virtually zero interest rates. That has driven up margins and made banks appear very profitable. The risk is that as interest starts to rise in any recovery and governments seek to exit from their bailouts, the banks will look a lot sicker than now. So either the top banks will stay on life support from the taxpayer, not lending to businesses and consumers but just to governments and financial markets, or their net results will fall.

Sciarretta: Eurozone banks have bigger losses to recognize than their U.S. counterparts, but they also have more means. Can we analyze this aspect?

McKee: Yes, as we explained, it is true that the ratio of losses admitted to losses forecast is much lower in Europe. But then, European banks have more capital and more assets. Eurozone banks have $24 trn in assets and $1.8 trn in tier-one capital; U.S. banks have $11.9 trn in assets and $1.1 trn in tier-one capital. And UK banks have $6.3 trn in assets and $600 bn in capital. So the situation in the Old Continent against the United States or the United Kingdom is not as bad as some claim. It is also true that European banks will take huge losses from any collapse in Eastern Europe, but our estimates for losses include that risk.

Sciarretta: Taken alone, what would be a range of losses with regard to Eastern European exposure?

McKee: We forecast as much as $250 bn in potential losses if Eastern European currencies crash and borrowers default on their mortgages and loans. But it seems the EU and the IMF are prepared to bail out potential defaulters in Eastern Europe, which, in turn, tempers the risk.

Sciarretta: Would you now discuss the leverage position in the American and European societies? After all, the panic of 2008 was rooted in too much debt. When collateral

values eroded (for instance, when house prices went down), both the economy and the markets plummeted.

McKee: U.S. national debt, both private and public, has not declined during this crisis. What has happened is that public-sector debt has rocketed upward to compensate for the fall in private-sector debt (both household and business).

Household debt remains some 15 percent above historic levels, business debt is 6 percent above, and financial sector debt is 14 percent above. U.S. household debt is now falling; but household assets, that is property values and stock values, have fallen much more. So household debt-to-wealth has risen to record highs!

Sciarretta: How will the consumer react?

McKee: Much more deleveraging must be done even if there is a pickup in the value of assets from here. It is the same story (if less pronounced) for the business sector. A problem is that with government net borrowing rocketing to nearly 15 percent of GDP, the private sector may be driven out of the market. Thus, any economic growth will be stunted. At the same time, as consumers and businesses continue to save more and spend less, private-sector growth will be correspondingly lower until balance sheets regain some equilibrium. U.S. households have raised their savings rates to about 4 percent of GDP from near zero and will probably have to hike them to about 8 percent of GDP, or government dissaving will put huge pressure on the U.S. dollar.

Sciarretta: And for Europe?

McKee: In the UK it is much the same story. Households need to cut back sharply on debt, as asset values have plunged; but so far the savings rate has not risen much. The big difference is that Eurozone households start with much larger savings ratios: about 10 to 15 percent of personal disposable income compared to 2 to 3 percent in the United States, UK, and Japan. So there is plenty of cushion to sustain consumption during any deleveraging. Further, Germanic economies (Germany, Austria, Switzerland) never had a housing bubble, and therefore household assets are less vulnerable on the downside.

Sciarretta: What are the implications when it comes to economic growth?

McKee: All this suggests that, contrary to consensus, the Eurozone is likely to recover quicker, and sustain higher growth and a stronger currency, than the United States or the UK, and the latest GDP figures tend to confirm this assumption.

Sciarretta: I have a question on the euro against the dollar: Since China is reluctant to let its currency go up, the dollar's weakness often materializes against the euro. How do you see this triangle—the United States, the Eurozone, and China?

McKee: It is clear that China is tired of financing America and being repaid with a depreciated currency. In fact, Beijing is rushing to buy real commodities beyond any production needs, it is shortening the duration of its holdings of U.S. Treasuries, it is getting out of agency debt, and it is proposing the substitution of the IMF's special drawing rights (SDRs) for the dollar as global reserve currency. It should be remembered that the makeup of the SDR is only 34 percent U.S. dollars, while 66 percent is other currencies such as the euro, the yen, and the pound.

Sciarretta: What do you expect?

McKee: Something has to give. Let's try to analyze the long-term perspective: At the end of 2008 China had $2.92 trn invested overseas, with about 70 percent of that invested in U.S.-dollar assets. Two-thirds of this wealth sits in the central banks. Now, if one considers that China's annual GDP is about $4.3 trn, it is easy to understand how the reserves are gigantic.

Sciarretta: You are suggesting that movements in the dollar have an ever-larger impact on China's accumulated wealth. Right?

McKee: Yes, a 1-percent loss in the value of China's dollar assets would wipe out wealth worth 0.67 percent of GDP and create a hole in the central bank's balance sheet.

Sciarretta: But if Beijing disgorges its dollars, the consequences may be disruptive.

McKee:	I could not agree more. If China stopped buying U.S. assets, the dollar would, of course, vanish. Yet, China would pay a very high price, because it relies on exports and has unprecedented reserves in dollars.
Sciarretta:	Is there a way out?
McKee:	The smartest thing Beijing could do would be to trade in as many of its dollars as possible to the IMF in return for the SDRs. They have already started to do so. In turn, the IMF could invest the dollars it does not need to bail out nations in difficulty by purchasing U.S. Treasuries and parking them at the Fed. In one of our reports, I have written that in this way everybody would be smiling, including, for a time, the markets. My point is that the dollar will decline, but not like a rock, because it is not in the interests of China.
Sciarretta:	How should people allocate their money with reference to the three areas: the Eurozone, Great Britain, and the United States?
McKee:	For all we have said, in the next three years, I favor the Eurozone over the United States and the UK. I would hold the euro versus the pound, greenback, and yen, with a target of 1.60 for the dollar/euro.
Sciarretta:	The same for bonds?
McKee:	Yes, Eurozone government bonds are better than U.S. Treasuries and UK gilts. Indeed, we even expect out-performance from bonds issued by state members such as Ireland or Greece. They experienced serious problems, and the problems enlarged the spread to German bunds. But all the state members have the protection of the euro and EU funding, if necessary. So the spreads will be tapering off.
Sciarretta:	Where would you position yourself in stocks?
McKee:	In equities, any global economic recovery will benefit Eurozone exporters, particularly in capital and industrial goods: This is where we would be overweight. Longer-term, alternative energy companies in Europe are especially well-placed, given the Eurozone commitment to funding global warming abatement and energy diversification.

Notes

Chapter 1: Euro versus Dollar

1. For a helpful discussion of the political and economic aspects of the birth and development of the euro see David Marsh, *The Euro: The Politics of the New Global Currency* (New Haven and London: Yale University Press, 2009).
2. The European Central Bank, the Eurosystem, and the European System of Central Banks, *The Road to Economic and Monetary Union*, 3rd ed. www.ecb.int/pub/pdf/other/escb_en_weben.pdf, April 2009.
3. Stephen S. Roach, Morgan Stanley Research, "Testing Time for Europe," New York, June 12, 2001; "L'élan de l'euro vis-à-vis du dollar ne devrait pas le mener bien loin," interview with Steve Hanke, Professor of Applied Economics, Johns Hopkins University, *Le Nouvel Économiste* (31 August 2001); Dresdner Bank, "Dresdner Bank Comments on Enlargement of European Union," London, June 2001.
4. Hans-Werner Sinn and Frank Westermann, National Bureau of Economic Research, "Why Has the Euro Been Falling? An Investigation into the Determinants of the Exchange Rate," Working Paper 8352 (July 2001).
5. David R. Kotok, "Italy-4 The Mafia" (June 27, 2001), accessed July 30, 2009. www.cumber.com/comments/062701.htm.
6. David R. Kotok, Cumberland Advisors, Inc., "The European e-paper: The Bearish Critics' Case vs. The Bullish Case (Ours)," www.cumber.com, July 9, 2001.
7. The International Monetary Fund, "Currency Composition of Official Foreign Exchange Reserves (COFER)," www.imf.org/external/np/sta/cofer/eng/index.htm, June 30, 2009.
8. Ibid.
9. Data depict domestic plus international debt outstanding but excluding financial intermediation debt; international debt securities by type, sector, and currency. Bank for International Settlements www.bis.org/statistics/secstats.htm, June 2009. (Note all data are quoted in U.S. dollars.)

10. Datastream International Limited. http://online.thomsonreuters.com/datastream/.

11. For details on policy, see ECB website and Christian Noyer, Vice President of the ECB, "Monetary Policy Formulation in the Euro Area," Conference of the NABE, May 21, 2001.

12. Antonio Polito, "An Interview with Wim Duisenberg, President of the European Central Bank." *La Republica* (June 27, 2001). www.cumber.com/Special/duisenberg.htm. Accessed July 30, 2009.

13. Bloomberg, May 28, 2008.www.bloomberg.com.

14. Alan Greenspan, "Reflections on Central Banking," at a symposium sponsored by the Federal Reserve Bank of Kansas City, Jackson Hole, Wyoming, August 26, 2005.

15. Ben Bernanke, Thomas Laubach, Frederic Mishkin, and Adam Posen, *Inflation Targeting: Lessons from the International Experience* (Princeton, NJ: Princeton University Press, 1999).

16. David R. Kotok, "Interview with Alessandro Pietrogiacomi, Lecturer for the University of Rome, Faculty of Economics and Commerce," June 11, 2001. www.cumber.com/Special/Answers.pdf. Accessed July 30, 2009.

17. David Hale, "Rebalancing the Global Economy," *Global Economics* 07 (09) (June 18, 2009).

18. Ibid.

19. Ibid.

20. *U.S. Economic Accounts*, U.S. Bureau of Economic Analysis. www.bea.gov/index.htm.

21. American Jobs Creation Act of 2004. www.natptax.com/2004jobactsummary.pdf.

Chapter 2: Convergence and Integration

1. Much of the factual information reported is found in many ECB reports (e.g., "10th Anniversary of the ECB," *The ECB Monthly Bulletin*, [June 2008]). www.ecb.int/pub/mb/html/index.en.html.

2. The 11 member states that had met the criteria for the adoption of the single currency were Austria, Belgium, Finland, France, Germany, Ireland, Italy, Luxembourg, the Netherlands, Portugal, and Spain. Five other members have joined in subsequent years—Greece on January 1, 2001, Slovenia in 2007, Cyprus and Malta in 2008, and Slovakia in 2009. Sweden has not fulfilled the conditions, and both Denmark and the UK were given the right to choose whether to adopt the euro and have both used the "opt-out" clause of not becoming part of the euro are for the time being. *Financial Integration in Europe* (ECB, April 2008). www.ecb.int/pub/pdf/mobu/mb200804en.pdf.

3. In 2008 the population of the euro area totaled 322 million, higher than 306 million in the United States and 127 million in Japan. Euro area GDP, measured in purchasing power parity terms, represents about 16 percent of global output, versus 21 percent in the United States and 6 percent in Japan. IMF data. www.imf.org/external/data.htm.

4. The Eurosystem (a) gives advice on the legislative and regulatory framework for the financial system and direct rule-making; (b) acts as a catalyst for private

sector activities by facilitating collective action; (c) enhances knowledge, raises awareness, and monitors the state of European financial integration; and (d) provides central bank services that also foster European financial integration. *Financial Integration in Europe* (ECB, April 2008). www.ecb.int/pub/pdf/mobu/mb200804en.pdf.

5. The Eurosystem seeks improving the efficiency of financial intermediation, cross-border provision of financial services, development and competition in financial services across countries and between new and older members.

6. Investment funds, insurance corporations, and pension funds tend to be well-diversified across countries and increasingly have become a major conduit for euro area households' funds, thereby pushing forward financial integration. The ECB report shows that from 1999 to 2007, investment funds have increased the percentage of their investment in foreign assets, including equity, from other euro area countries. When equity investment is considered, on average the fraction of portfolios invested in domestic equities has decreased from 42 percent at the end of 1998 to 32 percent by end-2007. *Financial Integration in Europe* (ECB, April 2008). www.ecb.int/pub/pdf/mobu/mb200804en.pdf.

7. In 2003, the ECB developed quantitative indicators. Both the standard deviation and coefficient of variation are based on interest rates across the euro area members and the EU member states and measure the trend towards the integration of financial markets. Both indicators are split in three sub-indicators: loans to households for house purchases, loans to nonfinancial corporations up to one year, and loans to nonfinancial corporations over one year. (Note that both Figures 2.5 and 2.6 depict loans up to one year.) *The European Commission Report* (ECB, 2003) and *Financial Integration in Europe* (ECB, April 2008) www.ecb.int/pub/pdf/mobu/mb200804en.pdf.

8. Kathleen Stephansen, "How U.S. Fiscal Policy Aids Both U.S. and Global Growth," in, Thomas R. Keene (Ed.), *Flying on One Engine: The Bloomberg Book of Master Market Economists* (New York: Bloomberg Press, September 13, 2005).

9. Ibid.

10. Ibid.

11. Ibid.

12. Ibid.

13. Jeffrey A. Frankel, "The Global Financial Crisis: A Selective Review of Recent Research in the International Financial and Macroeconomics Program," *NBER Reporter* 2 (2009), www.nber.org/reporter/2009number2/.

14. "Deconstructing Sovereign Ratings," Global Rates Strategy, Barclays Capital, July 17, 2009. www.scribd.com/doc/17514432/Barclays-Americas-Strategy-Report-71609, accessed on July 30, 2009.

15. "World Investment Prospects, Survey 2009–2011," Main results of an UNCTAD survey among large TNCs. (New York and Geneva: United Nations UNCTAD, July 22, 2009). www.unctad.org/en/docs/wips2008_en.pdf.

Chapter 3: Taxation

1. An example of the complexity can be found in the U.S. particular tax program known as the Alternative Minimum Tax (AMT). Under the AMT, 18 items are considered to be "preferences" and require a recomputation of taxes.

Essentially, that exposes taxpayers in the United States to two separate tax systems. Accountants and tax-return preparers are required to test taxation in both systems and then prepare the return for whichever one results in the higher tax. The AMT was originally designed as a special tax on very high-income individuals. In its first year it levied a tax on only 200 people with million-dollar-plus incomes. However, it has grown to be a very large tax and now impacts millions of taxpayers each year. In the case of capital gains, the issue becomes even more complex. Long-term capital gains are not preferences for the purpose of taxation under the AMT; however, they are an item that uses up the preference exemption. That means that an individual with long-term capital gains would be more likely to be subjected to the AMT because of those gains, and the AMT calculation would then be levied on the individual's other incomes. The AMT's top rate is 28 percent. This may seem to be less than the 35 percent top rate; however, under the AMT many items that are normally deductible in the regular tax mechanism are no longer deductible. A good example of this is state income taxes. High-tax states, like the example cited, New Jersey, often trigger AMT on their citizens because of the high state income taxes, which are considered to be a preference item. Let's take the case of a taxpayer in New Jersey who has a long-term capital gain. That taxpayer would incur, under normal taxation, a top rate of 15 percent under the federal long-term capital gain tax. In addition, the state of New Jersey would tax that capital gain at 10.75 percent, because the state of New Jersey does not treat long-term capital gains with any special lower rate. If the state income tax triggers AMT for the taxpayer, the calculation changes radically. The effect of the long-term capital gain would be to subject other portions of the taxpayer's income to the top bracket of 28 percent. In addition, the 10.75 percent paid on the long-term capital gain to the state of New Jersey would not be deductible for this taxpayer. In the end, the effective tax on the long-term capital gain could be as much as 28 percent tax and 10.75 percent to the state of New Jersey, for a total of 38.75 percent. Many taxpayers who enter capital-gains transaction planning find that their thought process is radically changed once they realize that what they thought would be a 15-percent tax transaction becomes a 38.75-percent transaction.

2. We base our comments on Deloitte, *International Tax and Business Guides* (2009).www.deloitte.com/view/en_PG/pg/insights-ideas/itbg/index.htm.
3. David Hale, "Has the U.S. Recession Ended?" *David Hale Global Economics* 7 (July 31, 2009), 11.

Chapter 4: Stock Market Evolution

1. Charles Mackay, *Extraordinary Popular Delusions & the Madness of Crowds.* (New York: Three Rivers Press, 1995); Charles P. Kindleberger, *Manias, Panics, and Crashes: A History of Financial Crises,* 5th ed. (Hoboken, NJ: John Wiley & Sons, 2005).
2. Elliot Posner, *The Origins of Europe's New Stock Markets* (Cambridge, MA: Harvard University Press, 2009).

3. William Witherell, "*International Exchange-Traded Funds (ETFs)—Austria,*" Cumberland Advisors. Retrieved April 27, 2006, from www.cumber.com/commentary.aspx?file=042706.asp.

Chapter 5: Accessing Europe with ETFs

1. *Standard & Poor's Indices Versus Active Funds Scorecard, Year End 2008,* April 20, 2009, p. 4. Based on an equal-weighted count of actively managed funds, measured against corresponding S&P benchmarks. Indexes are not investable and do not have expense ratios. Retrieved August 26, 2009, from http://www2.standardandpoors.com/spf/pdf/index/SPIVA_Report_Year-End_2008.pdf.
2. Ibid., p. 10.
3. William F. Sharpe, "The Arithmetic of Active Management," *Financial Analysts Journal,* 47(1) (1991), 7.
4. Investment Company Institute, "*2009 Investment Company Fact Book: A Review of Trends and Activity in the Investment Company Industry,*" p. 61. Retrieved August 26, 2009, from www.icifactbook.org/pdf/2009_factbook.pdf.
5. Barclays Global Investors, "*Why Taxes Matter—and What You Can Do about It.*" Retrieved August 26, 2009, from http://us.ishares.com/topics/tax_efficiency.htm;jsessionid=Oge8BhxMBl3r46F9m315kA**.isharescom-pra2?c=HFW98.
6. Morgan Stanley North America, "Exchange-Traded Funds Quarterly Report" (New York: August 11, 2009), p. 1.

Chapter 6: Successful Strategies in the Eurozone

1. Perhaps the "bible" in this field is James P. O'Shaughnessy, *What Works On Wall Street,* 3rd ed. (New York: McGraw-Hill, 2005.) The author illustrates the backtesting of a large number of single-factor and multi-factor strategies applied to U.S. stocks from 1952 through 2003. It would be unfair to summarize such an outstanding work in a few skimpy sentences, and the reader is warmly recommended to obtain the book. However, generally speaking, O'Shaughnessy found that stocks with low price-to-book, price-to-cashflow, price-to-sales, or price-to-earnings ratios did dramatically better than stocks with correspondingly high ratios. He also proved that stocks with low price-to-book, price-to-sales, or price-to-cashflow ratios tended to deliver higher annual rates of return than the market averages, but with higher volatility, so that on a risk-adjusted basis the results were mixed (better if the benchmark was formed by a universe of large stocks). Equally significant, O'Shaughnessy noted that by combining low price-to-book, price-to-sales, and price-to-earnings ratios with high relative strength, the performance of the portfolios vastly improved, beating the benchmarks both on a simple annual-return basis and on a volatility-adjusted basis. Of course, the book offers much more to the reader, and the only way to unveil its treasures is by reading it.

Chapter 7: Valuation

1. Teun Draaisma, Ronan Carr, Graham Secker, Edmund Ng, Matthew German, "Valuation Gap Europe Versus US Close to 35-year Low" (London: Morgan Stanley Research, June 22, 2009).

2. Bank of America—Merrill Lynch Research, *Fund Manager Survey Global* (March 18, 2009), www.ml.com/index.asp?id=7695_7696_8149_113521_113613_11361 4. In 2005–2007 the net percentage of global managers overweighting Europe was steadily above 30 percent. Early in 2009, global managers decisively shifted to an underweighting position.

3. Ibid.

4. Our estimates based on mutual fund national associations data.

5. Citigroup, "European Equity Strategy," July 30, 2009.

6. Ibid.

7. Boston Fed's "Monthly Mutual Funds." www.bos.frb.org/economic/mmfr/mmfr2007/jun2007.pdf, accessed August 31, 2009. June 2007. The ratio of Total Assets World Equity Funds to Total Assets Equity Funds is calculated by the Investment Company Institute, 1401 H St., NW, Washington, DC 20005. The higher the ratio, the larger the allocation abroad. It reached a top of around 26 percent early in 2008 and then declined to about 23 percent late in 2008 and early in 2009 (as we write, data are available until June 2009).

   World Equity Funds are the sum of the following four categories: 1. Emerging Markets Funds: invest primarily in companies based in various less-developed regions of the world. 2. Global Equity Funds: invest primarily in equity securities traded worldwide, including equity securities of U.S. companies. 3. International Equity Funds: must invest at least two-thirds of their portfolios in equity securities of companies located outside the United States. 4. Regional Equity Funds: invest in companies that are based in a specific part of the world, such as Europe, Latin America, the Pacific Region, or specific countries.

   Equity Funds are the sum of the following three categories: A. Capital Appreciation Funds: including aggressive growth funds, growth funds, and sector funds. B. World Equity Funds: including (1) through (4) listed above. C. Total Return Funds: including growth and income funds and income equity funds.

8. Factset estimates on Morningstar data. www.factset.com/subscription. Accessed August 31, 2009.

9. Stephen Jen, "US Dollar, The Biggest Dollar Diversifiers Are American," London, Morgan Stanley Research. July 19, 2007.

10. Greenwich Associates, April 2008, as presented by William Clark, Director of Investment State of New Jersey, to a Global Interdependence Conference in Paris on May 13, 2008.

11. Bank of America—Merrill Lynch Research, op. cit.

12. BCA Research, European Investment Strategy, July 12, 2009. www.bcaresearch.com.

13. Garfield Reynolds and Wes Goodman, "Pimco Says Dollar to Weaken as Reserve Status Erodes." Retrieved August 19, 2009, from Bloomberg.com. www.bloomberg.com/apps/news?pid=newsarchive&sid=aCM5WaqsP.98.

   Warren E. Buffett, "The Greenback Effect," *New York Times* (August 19, 2009). http://warrenbuffett.valuestockplus.net/the-greenback-effect.

14. Will and Ariel Durant, "Socialism and History," in *The Lessons of History* (New York: Simon and Schuster, 1968), pp. 60–61.

Chapter 8: Old Continent Stocks and the Super-Euro

1. "Global Exposure Guide 2007," November 16, 2007. A weak dollar phase was defined as a period without a 10-percent dollar rally. London: Morgan Stanley Research, Euroletter by Teun Draaisma, Graham Secker, Ronan Carr, Edmund Ng, Charlotte Swing, Matthew Garman.
2. Our estimates on data from Eurostat and the Bureau of Economic Analysis. http/epp.eurostat.ec.europa.eu/portal/page/portal/statistics/search_database and www.bea.gov/index.htm.
3. HSBC note, June 10, 2009.
4. Morgan Stanley, European Strategy, London, September 29 2008.
5. Gary Shilling's Insight, August 2009. www.agarysshilling.com/insight.html.
6. Global Exposure Guide, op. cit.
7. For instance, in the Morgan Stanley study cited in endnote 1, a 10-percent fall in the dollar was associated with an estimated decline of 3.1 percent in 2008 European earnings.

Chapter 9: When It Is America That Diversifies Out of the Dollar

1. The conference was organized by the Global Interdependence Center (Paris, May 13, 2008). Serious investors may want to take a look at the organization, of which the co-author of this book, David Kotok, is program chair. www.interdependence.org/. William Clark's presentation was titled "Strategic Impact of Currency Risk on U.S. Institutional Investors."
2. According to Greenwich Associates, the asset mix of U.S. pension funds augmented the share of alternative investments in the last few years. Equity real estate rose from 3.9 percent in 2005 to 4.9 percent in 2008, private equity moved from 3.6 to 5.4 percent, and hedge funds from 1.9 to 3.3 percent.

Chapter 10: Yes, Europe Is Cheaper than the United States (and the Gap Is Not Justified any Longer)

1. According to a Morgan Stanley report that this book quoted earlier (Morgan Stanley, *European Strategy*). Calculations looked at Europe, including the UK. 2009 net debt-to-equity for Europe ex financials was 58 percent versus 44 percent for the United States. However, five out of nine nonfinancial European sectors had lower debt ratios than their U.S. peers. Outside technology and health care, where the United States showed a marked advantage, cumulative gearing levels were quite similar.

Chapter 11: Europe-Asia: The Promising Linkage

1. *GloomBoomDoom*. Marc Faber Limited. www.gloomboomdoom.com, accessed August 31, 2009. I provided the website; Marc Faber publishes the report monthly.

Chapter 12: Eastern Europe: The Prognosis Looks Favorable

1. As of August 31, 2009, the top 10 holdings for the Templeton Eastern Europe Fund were as follow: (1) Turkiye Vakiflar (10.36 percent of the portfolio), a bank in Turkey. (2) Egis Nyrt (8.96 percent), a Hungarian group whose principal activities are the production and sales of pharmaceutical raw materials. (3) OTP Bank (7.41 percent), the largest commercial bank in Hungary, operating in Central and Eastern Europe. (4) CTC Media (6.39 percent), a leading media company in Russia. (5) Lukoil Holdings (5.99 percent), Russia's oil giant. (6) Erste Bank (5.18 percent), a retail bank, based in Vienna, Austria. It has a vast exposure to Central and Eastern Europe. (7) Turkiye Is Bankasi (4.68 percent), Turkey's first public bank. (8) Kazmunaigas Exploration Production (4.47 percent), an oil and gas company operating in the Republic of Kazakhstan. (9) OMV AG (3.61 percent), Austria's biggest oil and gas company, with important activities in other Central European countries. (10) Polnord (3.3 percent), a construction company and developer in Poland. Stocks in a portfolio continually change. A reader can have a sense of Dr. Mobius' current positions from Templeton's publicly disclosed fund holdings, posted on their website, www.franklintempleton.co.uk/uk/jsp_cm/funds/all_factsheets.jsp.

Chapter 14: For Now I Go with Continental Europe

1. Kenneth Fisher, "1980 Revisited," *Forbes* (March 3, 2000). www.forbes.com/columnists/free_forbes/2000/0306/6506186a.html, accessed September 14, 2009.

Chapter 15: Looking for Gems in the Eurozone Bond Market

1. Peter Temin, "A Market Economy in the Early Roman Empire," (February 2001). http://papers.ssrn.com/sol3/papers.cfm?abstract_id=260995. Accessed September 14, 2009.
2. Ibid.
3. Keynote address by Jean-Claude Tichet, President of the European Central Bank at the National Association of Business Economics, Philadelphia, October 5, 2004.
4. The yield curve of a debt instrument is the relationship between the interest rate and the time to maturity. For instance, if each successively longer-term maturity offers a higher yield than a shorter-term maturity, the yield curve traces a continually rising slope on a graph.
5. Three widely followed theories have evolved that attempt to explain the steepness of the curve:
   1. The Pure Expectations Theory holds that the slope of the yield curve reflects only investors' expectations for future short-term interest rates. Much of the time, investors expect interest rates to rise in the future, which accounts for the usual upward slope of the yield curve.
   2. The Liquidity Preference Theory, an offshoot of the Pure Expectations Theory, asserts that long-term interest rates not only reflect investors' assumptions

about future interest rates but also include a premium for holding long-term bonds, called the term premium or the liquidity premium. This premium compensates investors for the added risk of having their money tied up for a longer period, including the greater price uncertainty. Because of the term premium, long-term bond yields tend to be higher than short-term yields, and the yield curve slopes upward.

3. The Preferred Habitat Theory, another variation on the Pure Expectations Theory, states that in addition to interest-rate expectations, investors have distinct investment horizons and require a meaningful premium to buy bonds with maturities outside their "preferred" maturity, or habitat. Proponents of this theory believe that short-term investors are more prevalent in the fixed-income market, and therefore, longer-term rates tend to be higher than short-term rates.

Chapter 16: The Path of Least Resistance Leads to a Stronger Euro and a Weaker Dollar

1. The elasticity of imports with respect to U.S. GDP is larger than the same for exports. That usually causes the trade deficit to expand when economies are growing, but it serves as a contracting mechanism when economies are braking. In addition, with so much trade being in intermediate products for the supply chain, when world demand falls, so do both exports and imports.

Chapter 17: Eurozone Stocks: When Optimism Prevails

1. La société Alpha Mining. www.alphamining.com
2. Irving Fisher, *The Debt-Deflation Theory of Great Depressions.* (New York: Econometrica, 1933). http://fraser.stlouisfed.org/docs/meltzer/fisdeb33.pdf.
3. Readers interested in Kondratieff waves can find a large bibliography, including Chevallier's book *Greenspan's Taming of the Wave* (London: Kogan Page, 2000). The basic principle is that economic cycles alternate long periods of high and low growth, drawing a sinusoidal path that generally lasts 50 or 60 years before repeating itself in a similar way. Nikolai Kondratieff was the Russian economist who first brought these empirical observations to an international public.

Chapter 18: The Credit Crunch Fallout Is Dreadful Everywhere (but the Eurozone Can Survive)

1. See two Independent Strategy reports: "Credit Crunch: The Hit to the Liquidity Pyramid," November 15, 2007; and "Not Halfway Through!" February 27, 2008. www.instrategy.com.
2. International Monetary Fund, 30 September 2009. The same organization put the total amount at $4.1 trn in its "Global Financial Stability Review" of April 2009. www.imf.org.
3. Bloomberg, code WDCI. The International Monetary Fund, on 30 September 2009, said losses amounted to $1.3 trn through the first half of 2009.
4. Ibid.

About the Authors

David R. Kotok

David R. Kotok is the Chairman and Chief Investment Officer of Cumberland Advisors, an independent investment advisory firm that manages over $1.3 billion in individual and institutional separate accounts. He cofounded the firm in 1973 and has guided its investment strategy from inception. The firm specializes in capital preservation while managing risk and reward. The actively managed portfolios include municipal and taxable bonds as well as diversified global equities using exchange-traded funds.

Mr. Kotok maintains an active global presence as the Program Chairman of the Global Interdependence Center (GIC), a Philadelphia-based global trade and monetary policy group. In addition to numerous conferences held in the United States, he has also chaired premier investment and monetary conferences and delegations in France, Czech Republic, Ireland, Singapore, Israel, Chile, South Africa, Estonia, Vietnam, and Zambia.

Mr. Kotok's articles and financial market commentary have appeared in the *New York Times*, the *Wall Street Journal*, *Barron's*, and other publications. He is a frequent contributor to CNBC programs, including *Closing Bell, Morning Call, Power Lunch, Kudlow & Company, Squawk on the Street, Squawk Box Asia, Street Signs*, and *Worldwide Exchange*.

Mr. Kotok is a member of the National Business Economics Issues Council (NBEIC), the National Association for Business Economics (NABE), the Philadelphia Council for Business Economics

(PCBE), and the Philadelphia Financial Economists Group (PFEG). He has also served as a Commissioner of the Delaware River Port Authority (DRPA), on the Treasury Transition Teams for New Jersey governors Kean and Whitman, on the board of the New Jersey Economic Development Authority, and as Chairman of the New Jersey Casino Reinvestment Development Authority.

Mr. Kotok holds a BS degree in Economics from The Wharton School as well as dual master's degrees from the University of Pennsylvania.

Vincenzo Sciarretta

Vincenzo Sciarretta is a practicing financial journalist based in Italy. He has worked for *Milano Finanza,* the leading weekly financial magazine in Italy, and for *Borsa & Finanza,* a financial weekly similar to *Barron's* in the United States. He has been a contributor to the Economist Intelligence Unit, the research and intelligence unit of publishing company The Economist Group. He runs the website www.yeswetrade.com, devoted to individual investors.

Mr. Sciarretta has covered the European and international financial markets for the last 12 years. In addition to his journalistic efforts, Mr. Sciarretta has a background in technical analysis of stocks and commodities. As a technical analyst, he introduced new formulas relative to moving averages that are used by trend-following traders. He has published his work in leading journals such as *Futures* and *Technical Analysis of Stocks and Commodities.* He has also presented his work in Frankfurt, Germany; Milan, Italy; Chicago; Philadelphia; and other locations.

Mr. Sciarretta lives in Sirmione, a beautiful village on Lake Garda, about halfway between Venice and Milan.

Index